MW01259967

EASTER
PUZZLES

Publications International, Ltd.

Let's get social!
 @Publications_International
 @PublicationsInternational
 @BrainGames.TM
www.pilbooks.com

EGG-STRA SPECIAL PUZZLING

Get the whole family even more excited to celebrate the season with **Brain Games® Easter Puzzles**. Enjoy a collection of over 150 anagrams, crosswords, cryptograms, mazes, quizzes, word searches, and more!

Test your memory with accounts of Easter traditions around the world, like Bermuda's kite-flying festivities or Poland's Wet Monday, or complete the quotes from literature's most beloved bunny stories: *The Tale of Peter Rabbit* by Beatrix Potter and *The Adventures of Peter Cottontail* by Thornton W. Burgess. Discover the stories behind Easter Guinness World Records, and match the delicious Easter dish to its country of origin.

From centuries-old springtime traditions to the candy-filled baskets of today, **Brain Games® Easter Puzzles** promises to deliver on some springtime fun! If you find yourself stuck, answers can be found in the back of the book.

LARGEST CHOCOLATE EGG

Cryptograms are messages in substitution code. Break the code to read the message. For example, THE SMART CAT might become FVO QWGDF JGF if **F** is substituted for **T**, **V** for **H**, **O** for **E**, and so on.

Rfl feaej pej vjlzrdak rfl bejht'y hzjklyr vfevehzrl

Lzyrlj lkk ea tdyghzx kely re eal vfevehzrdlj da

Reyvz, Drzhx. lztl zr rfl Hl Zvvdzdljdl Yfeggdak

Vlarjl da 2011, rfl veaplvrdealjx lkk ilzysjlt

34 pllr, 1.05 davfly rzhh; fzt z vdjvsipljlavl ep

64 pllr, 3.65 davfly zr dry bdtlyr gedar; zat

bldkflt z bfeggdak 15,873 gesaty. Re gsr rfzr

dare gljyglvrdql, rfzr'y ylqljzh fsatjlt gesaty

flzqdlj rfza z pshh-kjeba izhl Zpjdvza yzqzaazf

lhlgfzar. Da zttdrdea re mldak rfl bejht'y hzjklyr

vfevehzrl lkk, dr zhye fehty rfl rdrhl zy rfl

bejht'y rzhhlyr.

Answers on page 174.

EASTER ANAGRAM

The following phrases are all anagrams for the same term related to Easter. What is it?

ANNOY CLOTH CUBE

NYLON TUBE COACH

UNBLEACH TYCOON

COMPLETE THE TALE

Below is a group of words that, when properly arranged in the blanks, reveal a quote from *The Tale of Peter Rabbit* by Beatrix Potter.

fir-tree   four   Mother   sand-bank   very

Once upon a time there were ____ little Rabbits, and their

names were—Flopsy, Mopsy, Cotton-tail, and Peter. They

lived with their ____ in a ____, underneath the root of a ____

big ____.

Answers on page 174.

SIGNS OF SPRING

Every word listed is contained within the group of letters. Words can be found in a straight line horizontally, vertically, or diagonally. They may read either forward or backward. The leftover letters reveal a quote from a comedian that will surely put a spring in your step.

APRIL	ICE MELTS
BALD EAGLES	INSECTS
BEARS AWAKEN	MIGRATIONS
BUDS	NESTS
BUTTERFLIES	PUDDLES
EARTHWORMS	RAIN
EQUINOX	ROBIN
FLOWERS	SHOWERS
FROGS	SOIL THAWS
GRAY WHALES	TULIPS
HUMMINGBIRDS	UMBRELLAS

Leftover letters:

_____

```
B S M R O W H T R A E S H P
U A S R E W O H S R I N U X
T L N G I L N S D N A T M O
T L E U R E I I U S B W M N
E E S A Y O F R B S E A I I
R R T Y I N G L P O A A N U
F B S E L A H W Y A R G G Q
L M I G R A T I O N S E B E
I U S E L G A E D L A B I T
E S P S R E W O L F W P R A
S O I L T H A W S R A R D T
S T L E M E C I Y O K R S O
B P U D D L E S I G E N W I
L L T I A S T C E S N I M S
```

Answers on page 174.

WORD LADDER

Change just one letter on each line to go from the top word to the bottom word. Do not change the order of the letters. You must have a common English word at each step.

LAMB

_____

_____

_____

_____

TAIL

Answers on page 174.

EASTER IN BERMUDA (PART I)

Read the story below, then turn the page and answer the questions.

On the island of Bermuda, Good Friday is celebrated with colorful kites taking to the skies. These homemade kites are constructed out of wooden sticks, string, and brightly-colored tissue paper. They include long cloth tails and are covered in intricate, geometric patterns. Traditionally, most kites are six- or eight-sided. They range in size, too: Some are small, but others are so large that they require multiple people to get them airborne. The kite design is completed using special glued tissues called "hummers." These help emit a buzzing or droning sound when caught in the warm Bermudian breeze.

No one is exactly sure what started this kite-flying tradition, although legend has it that it began when a local teacher had difficulty explaining the story of Jesus's resurrection to his Sunday school students. To provide a better visual of the act of rising into heaven, he launched a kite painted to look like Jesus into the sky.

The annual Kite Festival on Horseshoe Bay Beach is the perfect place to watch hundreds of kites dotting the skies. The display can be quite competitive, too: Prizes are awarded to the winners in a range of categories, including the smallest, largest, most beautiful, and most original kites. In addition to the kite-flying, visitors can also enjoy a bountiful supply of hot cross buns and codfish cakes.

EASTER IN BERMUDA (PART II)

(Do not read this until you have read the previous page!)

1. How many sides do Bermudian Easter kites typically have?
   - A. 4 or 6
   - B. 6 or 8
   - C. 8 or 10
   - D. 10 or 12

2. What is the name of the special tissues used to emit a noise as the kites fly?
   - A. buzzers
   - B. droners
   - C. hissers
   - D. hummers

3. Legend has it that Bermuda's kite-flying tradition began when a local teacher had trouble explaining the resurrection of Jesus.
   - _____ True
   - _____ False

4. What food can visitors to the annual kite festival on Horseshoe Bay Beach enjoy?
   - A. codfish cakes
   - B. fish chowder
   - C. rum cake
   - D. sweet potato pudding

Answers on page 174.

EASTER MAZE

Answer on page 174.

LARGEST EASTER EGG

Cryptograms are messages in substitution code. Break the code to read the message. For example, THE SMART CAT might become FVO QWGDF JGF if **F** is substituted for **T, V** for **H, O** for **E,** and so on.

Evuixufl ofurffs Exgci xsl Uxqqxmcsx vs eciudfqs

Wxuxgcsvx, Etxvs, udf TcquXafsuiqx udfkf

txqy ve yscrs zcq vue evh lvzzfqfsu rcqgle cz

xlafsuiqf, xe rfgg xe cafq 3 kvgfe cz qcggfq

wcxeufqe. Vu'e xgec yscrs zcq udf rcqgl'e

gxqmfeu Ifwcqxufl Fxeufq fmm, x uvugf rdvwd

vu eucgf zqck Xeecwvxwxc Avevuf Tckfqclf'e

fmm vs Tckfqclf, Oqxnvg, vs Kxqwd cz 2022.

Etxvs'e iskveexogf, kiguvwcgcqfl xuuqxwuvcs

zfxuiqfe x qxsmf cz oqvmdu ogif, mqffs,

qfl, pfggcr, xsl mcgl txuufqse. Vu euxsle xu

xttqchvkxufgp 52.43 zffu uxgg, xsl kfxeiqfe

34.94 zffu vs lvxkfufq. Rdvgf udf fmm ve

wfquxvsgp vktqfeevaf, vu'e fsuvqfgp vsflvogf.

Answers on page 174.

M_SS_NG V_W_LS

Below is a quote from *The Adventures of Peter Cottontail* by Thornton W. Burgess. The only thing is, some terms have lost A, E, I, O, and U, as well as any punctuation and spaces between words. Can you figure out the missing vowels and decipher each term?

"Peter Rabbit! Peter Rabbit! I don't see what MTHRNTR ever gave me such a CMMN sounding name as that for. People LGH at me, but if I had a fine sounding name they wouldn't laugh. Some folks say that a name doesn't amount to NYTHNG, but it does. If I should do some WNDRFL thing, nobody would think anything of it."

GARDEN ADDAGRAM

This puzzle functions exactly like an anagram with an added step: In addition to being scrambled, each term below is missing the same letter. Discover the missing letter, then unscramble the words. When you do, you'll reveal 5 terms associated with gardening.

ANCIENT WAG (two words)

BEWARE HOWL

KEA

LINK REPS

OWLET

Answers on page 175.

BLOSSOMING SHRUBS & TREES

Every word listed is contained within the group of letters. Words can be found in a straight line horizontally, vertically, or diagonally. They may be read either forward or backward.

ALMOND	PAWPAW
AZALEA	PEAR
BUCKEYE	PLUM
CHERRY	REDBUD
CRABAPPLE	SASSAFRAS
DAPHNE	SERVICEBERRY
DOGWOOD	SHADBUSH
FORSYTHIA	SILVERBELL
FOTHERGILLA	SNOW WREATH
FRINGE	SPICEBUSH
LILAC	VIBURNUM
MAGNOLIA	WILLOW

```
C J C B R P O U P A W P A W V R
H S I L V E R B E L L D T E U Q
E N E L I L A C T O C J R X I N
R O I R O R W I L L O W S Y A R
R W P P V I B U R N U M H A Z E
Y W E S P I C E B U S H H T W D
I R A O N E C R A B A P P L E B
S E R F O T H E R G I L L A W U
H A P O R D F O B U C K E Y E D
A T S R A D A R R E A U P L U M
D H X S Z R O P I S R L E S L J
B L L Y A C N G H N R R M O J I
U Z A T L F F L W N G U Y O S Q
S N E H E A R G G O E E M E N I
H D S I A V M A G N O L I A K D
E V I A V K E H S Z Z D V B Z Q
```

Answers on page 175.

SPRING SURPRISE

3 4
5
2
1 6
231 8 7 13
226 227
228 9
225 230
229
216 12 14
10 15
224 11 16
223
189 186
217 215 187 185 170 169
222 188 184 171 168
190 183 174 167
218 214 182 180 172 17
221 219 191 181 173
213 179 175 166
220 212 192 178 177 176 165
211 193 194 164 18
210 199 154 155 163 19
195 20
209 198 162 21
196 153
208 200 161 22
201 197 156
207 160 23
81 205 202 152 157 159 24
85 86 88 89 91 92 38
80 84 87 93 158 25
79 82 90 39
83 102 100 99 98 97 40
104 103 107 101 94 206 37 26
106 110 111 96 95 41 27
105 108 112 113 114 115 203 42 45 36
124 109 120 118 117 151 43 44 46 28
78 125 123 121 122 119 135 116 57 56 55 47
76 130 134 136 54
77 126 129 131 133 137 149 150 53 29
75 128 132 58 48 35 30
127 140 139 138 148 52 34 31
74 142 141 144 59 49 33 32
73 143 69 147 60
145 146
72 68 61
70 67 66 51
71 65 62 50
64 63

16 Answer on page 175.

EASTER EQUALS

You may be familiar with the Easter Bunny, but did you know that other places around the world have different animals and symbols that represent the arrival of Easter? Match the Easter symbol to its respective country.

1. Bilby

2. Cuckoo

3. Flying bells

4. Fox

5. Witch

A. Australia

B. France

C. Germany

D. Sweden

E. Switzerland

Answers on page 175.

BROKEN EGG

What number was painted on this egg before it was broken?

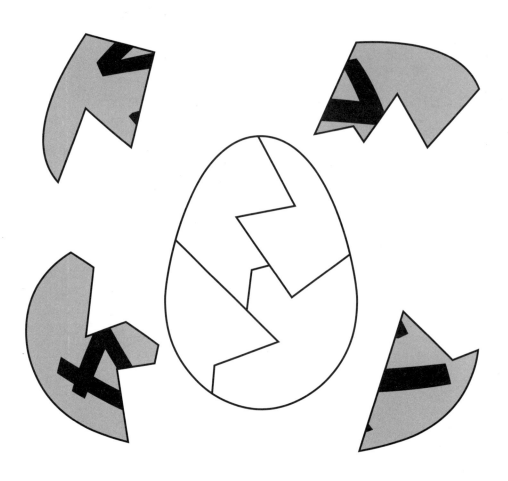

Answer on page 175.

WORD LADDER

Change just one letter on each line to go from the top word to the bottom word. Do not change the order of the letters. You must have a common English word at each step.

EASTER

_____

_____

_____

_____

_____

LILIES

Answers on page 175.

SEASONAL THEME

ACROSS

1. Skip a turn
5. Try a little of
10. Alaskan islander
12. Big name in aluminum
13. Come-ons
14. Big winds
15. Hare that leaves candy
17. Atlanta-to-Tampa dir.
18. "_____ lookin' at ya"
19. Bonnie's partner
21. Forty-niner's filing
23. Small battery size
26. They're often found at Easter
29. Allow in
30. Diarist Nin
31. River through Paris
32. Boxer's dream
33. Frisky swimmer
34. Active ingredient in Off!

DOWN

1. Loses color
2. "John Doe"
3. Taste or touch
4. Treat for winter birds
5. Like many manila folders
6. Appeal
7. Tea cake
8. Whistle-stops
9. Requiring no great labor
11. Lao-_____
16. Cat and hat, e.g.
19. Incisor neighbor
20. Seat on shafts
21. West Pointer
22. Word after speed or age
23. Kind of marble
24. Like a gymnast
25. Desirable quality
26. El _____, Texas
27. "Can't Help Lovin' _____ Man" ("Show Boat" song)
28. Oklahoma city

Answers on page 175.

PICTURE THIS

Place each of the 22 boxes in the 6 by 4 grid below so they form an Easter picture.
Do this without cutting the page apart: Use only your eyes.

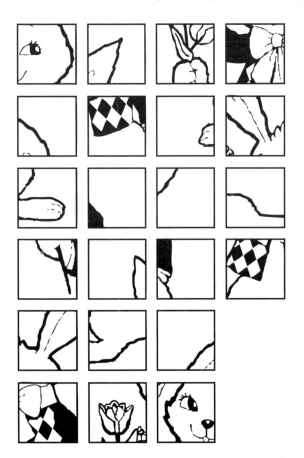

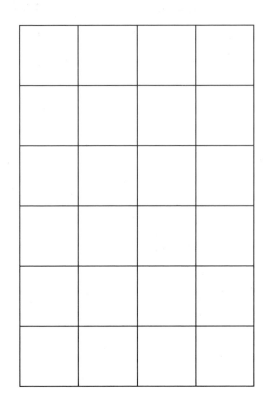

Answer on page 175.

WORD LADDER

Change just one letter on each line to go from the top word to the bottom word. Do not change the order of the letters. You must have a common English word at each step.

WARM

———

———

WIND

COMPLETE THE TALE

Below is a group of words that, when properly arranged in the blanks, reveal a quote from *The Tale of Peter Rabbit* by Beatrix Potter.

accident   fields   garden   lane   morning

"Now my dears," said old Mrs. Rabbit one ____, "you may

go into the ____ or down the ____, but don't go into Mr.

McGregor's ____: your Father had an ____ there; he was put

in a pie by Mrs. McGregor."

Answers on page 176.

SUDOKU

Use deductive logic to complete the grid so that each row, each column, and each 3 by 3 box contains the numbers 1 through 9 in some order. The solution is unique.

7		6			4			8
	1	4			5		6	
5	2		6	9		7		
	6	1		4	2			
		7				1		
			9	1		4	7	
		2		8	9		4	3
	5		2			8	9	
6			4			5		7

Answers on page 176.

LARGEST EASTER EGG HUNT

Cryptograms are messages in substitution code. Break the code to read the message. For example, THE SMART CAT might become FVO QWGDF JGF if **F** is substituted for **T**, **V** for **H**, **O** for **E**, and so on.

Pql lbb qdjp nw k xvkwwnx Lkwplz pzkunpnyj, kju tyz byyu zlkwyj: Xqnvuzlj vyel vyyinjb tyz qnuulj ulxyzkplu lbbw kju bkpqlznjb pqlc nj rkwilpw. Mqnvl wycl qdjpw zlfdnzl wlkzxqnjb pqzydbq k rkxihkzu, ypqlz qdjpw kzl vkzblz kju ckul tyz pql ljpnzl jlnbqryzqyyu py ljgyh. Rdp jlelz qkw pqnw rllj pkilj py wdxq kj lspzlcl kw yj Koznv 1, 2007, mqlj pql tyviw kp pql Xhozlww Bkzuljw Kueljpdzl Okzi nj Mnjplz Qkelj, Tvyznuk, pyyi np doyj pqlcwlvelw py yzbkjnal pql myzvu'w vkzblwp Lkwplz lbb qdjp. Kxxyzunjb py Bdnjjlww Myzvu Zlxyzuw, 9753 xqnvuzlj kju pqlnz okzljpw wlkzxqlu tyz k mqyoonjb 501,000 lbbw. Zdcyz qkw np pqkp k jdcrlz yt djunwxyelzlu lbbw cnbqp wpnvv rl qnunjb nj pql Kueljpdzl Okzi'w mnvulzjlww.

Answers on page 176.

EASTER ANAGRAM

The following phrases are all anagrams for the same term related to Easter. What is it?

GENT HUG

GET HUNG

NEG THUG

M_SS_NG V_W_LS

Below is a quote from *The Adventures of Peter Cottontail* by Thornton W. Burgess. The only thing is, some terms have lost A, E, I, O, and U, as well as any punctuation and spaces between words. Can you figure out the missing vowels and decipher each term?

"Cottontail, Peter Cottontail! How much better sounding that is than Peter Rabbit! That sounds as if I really was SMBDY. Yes, Sir, that's the very name I want. Now I must send word to all my FRNDS that HRFTR I am no longer Peter Rabbit, but Peter Cottontail." Peter KCKD up his heels in just the funny way he always does when he is PLSD.

Answers on page 176.

PIC-A-PIX

Use the clues on the left of every row and the top of every column to reveal the picture hidden in the grid below. Numbers indicate how many blocks get colored in, and the sequence in which they get colored. There must be at least one empty square between each sequence.

Column clues (top to bottom):

C1	C2	C3	C4	C5	C6	C7	C8	C9	C10	C11	C12	C13	C14	C15
			1			2								
		1	1	2	1	1	2	2						
		2	2	1	2	2	1	3					2	
	2	1	1	1	1	1	1	1	4	1			1	
	1	1	2	1	2	2	1	2	1	4	1		1	7
5	2	1	1	1	1	1	1	1	4	4	5	3	1	1

Row clues (left of each row):

Row	Clues
1	4 1 3
2	1 2 4
3	1 2 1 1
4	1 1 1 1 2 2
5	10 1
6	1 1 1 1 4 2
7	1 1 2 1
8	2 1 1 1 1 1 1
9	1 1 1 1 1 2 1
10	1 3
11	10
12	1 1 2 3
13	1 1 1 1
14	1 1
15	4

Answer on page 176.

GARDEN TOOLS

Every word listed is contained within the group of letters. Words can be found in a straight line horizontally, vertically, or diagonally. They may be read either forward or backward.

AERATOR	PRUNER
AXE	RAKE
BULB PLANTER	SAW
COMPOST BIN	SHEARS
DIBBER	SHOVEL
GARDEN FORK	SPADE
GLOVES	SPRINKLER
HATCHET	THORN STRIPPER
HOE	TROWEL
HOSE	WATERING CAN
KNEELER	WEEDER
LAWN MOWER	WHEELBARROW
LEAF BLOWER	WIDGER
LOPPER	WROTTER

```
P W H E E L B A R R O W G Q W
V T B L Z P E G B S H E A R S
H O E U S P R I N K L E R T H
O A E G L O V E S A W M D H O
S L T S D B C X H J Z D E O V
E E O C O M P O S T B I N R E
B A T P H M K L O C K B F N L
W F D R P E A N A X E B O S Z
R B A U O E T P E N A E R T W
O L A N C W R R R E T R K R E
T O J E S M E M A T L E D I E
T W L R P O R L T Q G E R P D
E E K L A W N M O W E R R P E
R R W I D G E R R A K E B E R
N W A T E R I N G C A N I R J
```

Answers on page 176.

COMPLETE THE TALE

Below is a group of words that, when properly arranged in the blanks, reveal a quote from *The Tale of Peter Rabbit* by Beatrix Potter.

blackberries   currant   mischief   naughty   umbrella

"Now run along, and don't get into ____. I am going out."
Then old Mrs. Rabbit took a basket and her ____, and went
through the wood to the baker's. She bought a loaf of
brown bread and five ____ buns. Flopsy, Mopsy, and Cottontail, who were good little bunnies, went down the lane to
gather ____: But Peter, who was very ____, ran straight away
to Mr. McGregor's garden, and squeezed under the gate!

   Answers on page 176.

EASTER IN THE CZECH REPUBLIC (PART I)

Read the story below, then turn the page and answer the questions.

The morning of Maundy Thursday, called "Green Thursday" in the Czech Republic, is the last time you'll hear church bells ring throughout the country until Holy Saturday, or "White Saturday." It is said that the souls of the bells fly off to Rome to be blessed by the Pope. During this time, people take the opportunity to receive the bells' last blessings, shaking trees in their gardens to guarantee a good harvest or jiggling coins in their hand to ensure prosperity.

Despite the silent bells, however, Holy Week is not exactly a quiet affair. In Moravia, a historical region in the east of the Czech Republic, groups of young boys take to the streets vigorously shaking traditional wooden noisemakers. Called *řehtačka*, these rattles are traditionally used to call people to church service during the bells' silence. The noise is also thought to scare away Judas Iscariot, the disciple who betrayed Jesus, and prevent him from harming the community.

The procession of noisy boys is repeated again on Good Friday, and then again on White Saturday. On this day, however, their progress is slowed: The boys go from door to door, stopping at every house to twirl their noisemakers until they receive a present, usually money. Then, they divide their earnings among themselves.

EASTER IN THE CZECH REPUBLIC (PART II)

(Do not read this until you have read the previous page!)

1. Instead of Maundy Thursday, the Thursday before Easter in the Czech Republic goes by which other name?
    - A. Good Thursday
    - B. Green Thursday
    - C. Red Thursday
    - D. White Thursday

2. Where do the souls of the bells go?
    - A. Florence
    - B. Genoa
    - C. Rome
    - D. Vatican City

3. What is the name of the historical region of the Czech Republic that uses *řehtačka* noisemakers?
    - A. Bohemia
    - B. Moravia
    - C. Prague
    - D. Silesia

4. On White Saturday, the group of young boys go from door to door to twirl their noisemakers in exchange for a present, which they then share.
    - _____ True
    - _____ False

Answers on page 176.

EASTER MAZE

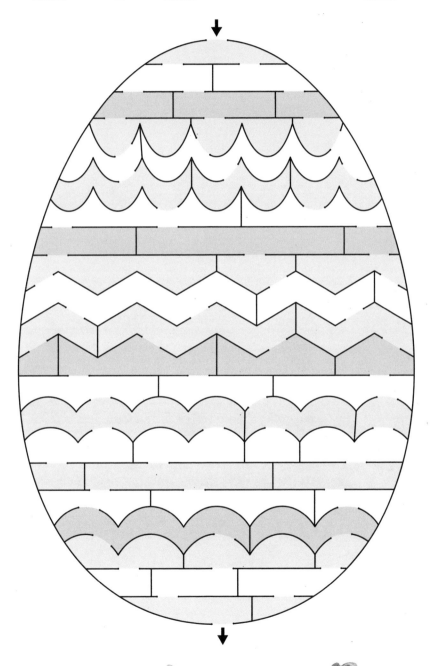

Answer on page 177.

A SPRING BOUQUET

Every word listed is contained within the group of letters. Words can be found in a straight line horizontally, vertically, or diagonally. They may be read either forward or backward.

ALLIUM	HYACINTH
ANEMONE	IRIS
ASTILBE	LILAC
CARNATION	LILY OF THE VALLEY
DAFFODIL	MUSCARI
DAISY	PEONY
EASTER LILY	RANUNCULUS
FORGET-ME-NOT	ROSE
FREESIA	SWEET PEA
HELLEBORE	TULIP

```
D H K X X Z N K R M B L H W R S
K R O H I V A S T I L B E C Y D
K O R M I R H Y A C I N T H Y R
X S J M M L I L A C L D G H C V
K E I E T R G S Y F Y A M B W E
F N O U U D P C O A O N S R L A
R O J M L A E A M H F E W A V S
E N Q I I F O R G E T M E N O T
E Q B A P F N N D L H O E U L E
S I M C O O Y A A L E N T N D R
I A U O R D I T I E V E P C L L
A K S N E I S I S B A P E U H I
I B C F P L H O Y O L T A L F L
L D A I L Z O N B R L R K U E Y
A I R A L H D Y G E E M B S I F
R C I A L L I U M F Y F A Y G F
```

Answers on page 177.

WORD LADDER

Change just one letter on each line to go from the top word to the bottom word. Do not change the order of the letters. You must have a common English word at each step.

HOLY

____

____

____

____

WEEK

Answers on page 177.

LARGEST EASTER EGG TREE

Cryptograms are messages in substitution code. Break the code to read the message. For example, THE SMART CAT might become FVO QWGDF JGF if F is substituted for T, V for H, O for E, and so on.

Rlx rqgbjrjiw is bxeiqgrjwt Xgvrxq xtt rqxxv lgv qiirv tijwt mgez ri Txqagwp, olxqx siq exwrfqjxv xttv lgux mxxw lfwt iw mqgwelxv is ifrbiiq rqxxv gwb mfvlxv fvjwt qjmmiw gwb rlqxgb. Rlx rqgbjrjiw, egnnxb *lvrxqxjxqmgfa*, jv wi niwtxq njajrxb ri yfvr Txqagwp, lioxuxq. Iw Agqel 16, 2017, gw Xgvrxq xtt rqxx eiwvjvrjwt is 82,404 hgjwrxb lxw xttv ogv geljxuxb mp Gvviejgegi Ujvjrx Hiaxqibx ri exnxmqgrx lvrxqsxvr jw Hiaxqibx, Vgwrg Egrgqjwg, Mqgcjn. Qxhiqrxbnp, jr riiz gnaivr gw xwrjqx pxgq ri einnxer xwiftl xttvlxnnv ri bxeiqgrx rlx rqxx gwb vxefqx rlx Tfjwwxvv Oiqnb Qxeiqb.

EASTER ANAGRAM

The following phrases are all anagrams for the same term related to Easter. What is it?

ESTUARY SEDAN

STAY UNDERSEA

UNRATED ESSAY

COMPLETE THE TALE

Below is a group of words that, when properly arranged in the blanks, reveal a quote from *The Tale of Peter Rabbit* by Beatrix Potter.

beans   cucumber   meet   radishes   sick

First he ate some lettuces and some French ____; and then

he ate some ____; And then, feeling rather ____, he went to

look for some parsley. But round the end of a ____ frame,

whom should he ____ but Mr. McGregor!

Answers on page 177.

WORD LADDER

Change just one letter on each line to go from the top word to the bottom word. Do not change the order of the letters. You must have a common English word at each step.

WINDY

_____

_____

_____ (currency of South Africa)

_____

_____

RAINY

SPRING CLEANING

Every word listed is contained within the group of letters. Words can be found in a straight line horizontally, vertically, or diagonally. They may be read either forward or backward.

CHANGE AIR FILTER

CHANGE LINENS

CLEAN OUT FRIDGE

DECLUTTER

DEEP CLEAN OVEN

DEFROST FREEZER

DISCARD OLD SPICES

DUST CEILING

OIL HINGES

OPEN WINDOWS

ORGANIZE

POLISH SILVER

ROTATE MATTRESS

SCRUB TOILET

SHAMPOO RUGS

SOAK COFFEEPOT

SWEEP

SWITCH OUT DECOR

VACUUM

WASH MIRRORS

WASH WINDOWS

WAX FLOORS

WIPE APPLIANCES

WIPE WALLS

```
W D I S C A R D O L D S P I C E S V
I O R G A N I Z E C B H R P D W S W
P S D D S C S Q G H J S W O U W O I
E W E E C H W L Q A J H A L S A A P
A E F E R A I D I N O A S I T S K E
P E R P U N T E O G O M H S C H C W
P P O C B G C C P E I P M H E W O A
L S S L T E H L E A L O I S I I F L
I W T E O L O U N I H O R I L N F L
A A F A I I U T W R I R R L I D E S
N X R N L N T T I F N U O V N O E V
C F E O E E D E N I G G R E G W P A
E L E V T N E R D L E S S R I S O C
S O Z E T S C J O T S U X Z F K T U
U O E N T Y O X W E W B N P A M A U
E R R O I I R R S R Y W F G R V Z M
B S H M C L E A N O U T F R I D G E
R O T A T E M A T T R E S S J O P T
```

Answers on page 177.

EASTER MAZE

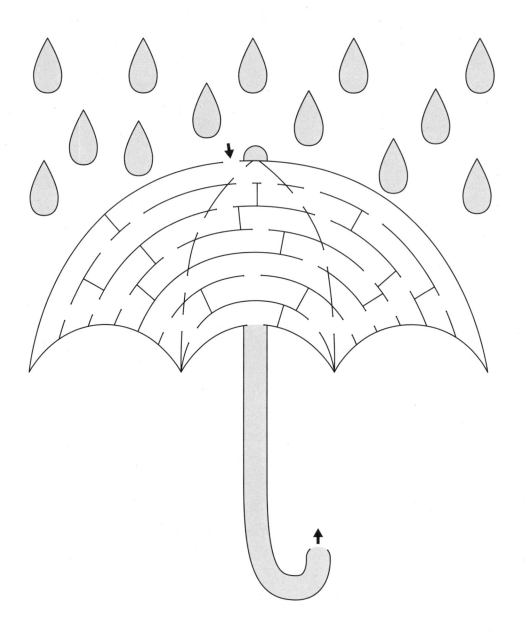

Answer on page 178.

EASTER IN FRANCE (PART 1)

Read the story below, then turn the page and answer the questions.

Although residents of Haux, a small town in the south of France, might reside in a town of only 800 people, they have quite the enormous Easter tradition. Every year on Easter Monday, the town cracks open more than 4500 eggs into a gigantic pan to create a massive omelet. The event takes place in the town's main square and can serve approximately 1000 people.

Bessières, another town in southern France, takes the delicious tradition one step further. Every year, the town puts on the Fête de l'Omelette Géante, a festival which combines three days of events—dinners, Easter egg hunts, parades, and performances—that culminate on Easter Monday with an even bigger omelet. Crowds gather in the streets to watch the monstrous omelet being made over a giant fire. Volunteers, about 50 or so, help crack over 15,000 eggs in preparation, while several local chefs come together to cook the omelet using giant wooden spoons that look more like oars. Thousands of people are served.

But what are the origins of such an odd tradition? According to legend, when French Emperor Napoleon Bonaparte and his army were traveling through the south of France, they stopped to rest in a small town and ate omelets. Napoleon reportedly enjoyed his omelet so much that, the next day, he ordered the townspeople to gather their eggs and create one giant omelet for him and his army to share.

Whatever its beginnings, the tradition has not only grown in egg count—it's also leapt borders. In addition to feeding several small French villages, the omelet has seen popularity across the ocean in Pigüé, Argentina.

EASTER IN FRANCE (PART II)

(Do not read this until you have read the previous page!)

1. About how many eggs are needed for the town of Haux to create their massive Easter omelet?
   A. 800
   B. 4500
   C. 11,500
   D. 15,000

2. The Fête de l'Omelette Géante festival in the town of Bessières lasts five whole days.
   _____ True
   _____ False

3. Approximately how many eggs are used to create Bessières' monstrous omelet?
   A. 800
   B. 4500
   C. 11,500
   D. 15,000

4. Napoleon reportedly ordered the townspeople of southern France to make two omelets: one for him, one for his army to share.
   _____ True
   _____ False

Answers on page 178.

M_SS_NG V_W_LS

Below is a quote from *The Adventures of Peter Cottontail* by Thornton W. Burgess. The only thing is, some terms have lost A, E, I, O, and U, as well as any punctuation and spaces between words. Can you figure out the missing vowels and decipher each term?

Reddy Fox, curled up behind the big pine stump, was dreaming of a coop full of CHCKNS, where there was no Bowser the Hound to watch over them. Suddenly something landed on him with a thump that knocked all his BRTH out. For an instant it FRGHTND Reddy so that he just shook and shook. Then he got his senses together and DSCVRD that it was Jimmy Skunk who had JMPD on him.

FLOWER ADDAGRAM

This puzzle functions exactly like an anagram with an added step: In addition to being scrambled, each term below is missing the same letter. Discover the missing letter, then unscramble the words. When you do, you'll reveal 5 terms associated with flowers that bloom in early spring.

A ZEAL

BED LIGHTENER (two words)

FID FOLD

FISHY ROT

HATCHING PREY (two words)

Answers on page 178.

MOST EXPENSIVE CHOCOLATE EGG

Cryptograms are messages in substitution code. Break the code to read the message. For example, THE SMART CAT might become FVO QWGDF JGF if F is substituted for T, V for H, O for E, and so on.

Nzk Xqtrkg Mbksjtkr Kxx ehmg'n nzk thvxkmn szqsqthnk kxx kfkv ahrk, own pn ehm skvnhpgtl nzk aqmn kubkgmpfk. Svkhnkr ol Epttpha Swvtkl hgr zpm nkha qd 6 szqsqthnpkvm, nzk bvpskl kxx ehm mswtbnkr kgnpvktl dvqa Hakrkp szqsqthnk, ezpsz wmkm sqsqh okhgm swtnpfhnkr pg nzk Szwhq vkxpqg qd Fkgkywkth. Pgmprk nzk kxx ekvk nvwddtkm hgr sqwnwvk szqsqthnkm, ezptk nzk qwnmprk ehm rksqvhnkr epnz 12 mahttkv szqsqthnk kxxm, 5 ezpnk dtqekvm, 20 apgp szqsqthnk ohvm, hgr xqtr tkhd. Pn nqqj nzvkk rhlm nq ahjk. Nzk Xqtrkg Mbksjtkr Kxx mqtr hn nzk Vqlht Sqwvnm qd Iwmnpsk, Tqgrqg, qg Ahvsz 20nz, 2012, dqv £7000. Pn ekpxzkr aqvk nzhg 110 bqwgrm, hgr ehm hbbvqupahnktl 3 dkkn, 6.13 pgszkm nhtt hgr 1 dqqn, 9.26 pgszkm eprk.

Answers on page 178.

THINK SPRING

Answer on page 178.

SPRING FRUIT

Every word listed is contained within the group of letters. Words can be found in a straight line horizontally, vertically, or diagonally. They may be read either forward or backward.

APRICOTS

BANANAS

BLUEBERRIES

CANTALOUPE

CHERRIES

CURRANTS

GRAPEFRUIT

HONEYDEW

KIWIS

KUMQUATS

LEMONS

LIMES

MANGO

MULBERRIES

ORANGES

PEACHES

PINEAPPLE

STRAWBERRIES

WATERMELON

```
V Y X L Q S S N S E I R R E H C
S A M O L T E G P B R W X T R C
D J S K E O I H B E U G O P H H
O A E L M C R K H M A N G O D S
P T I I O I R X H O G C S A F D
I T R M N R E P E D N E H U Q D
N I R E S P B F M H I E M E F A
E U E S K A E C B R M B Y U S P
A R B V I R U B R U W V C D Q X
P F L H W Y L E Z O R A N G E S
P E U H I V B G S A N A N A B W
L P M D S W A T E R M E L O N C
E A D C A N T A L O U P E E P W
W R U R O W R S T A U Q M U K O
H G T V C E Q E A L C Q E J J C
X S S T N A R R U C N D S T L T
```

Answers on page 178.

BROKEN EGG

What letter was painted on this egg before it was broken?

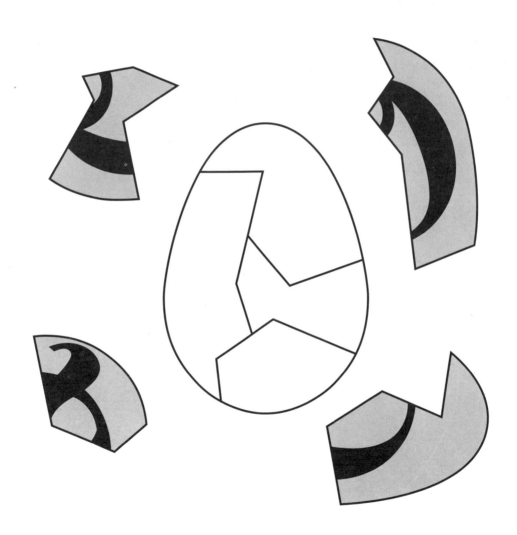

Answer on page 179.

EASTER EQUALS

Easter celebrations make use of several symbolic images. Match each symbol to the idea it represents.

1. Basket

2. Eggs

3. Easter lily

4. Lamb

5. Rabbit

A. Birds' nests

B. Fertility

C. Goodness; purity; sacrifice

D. Joy; motherhood; peace

E. New life; rebirth

Answers on page 179.

EASTER RIDDLES

ACROSS

1. Shaving lotion brand
5. Actor Milo
10. "SOS" pop group
14. Cherrystone, e.g.
15. Subatomic particles
16. Not the original color
17. What kind of exercise does the Easter Bunny do?
19. State in which seven presidents were born
20. Hams it up
21. Maze runners, often
23. "Steppenwolf" author
26. N.Y. Met, e.g.
27. Municipal trash venue
30. Items found in remote areas?
33. Folksinger Phil
34. Severely wounded
36. GI's dinner
37. Champagne choice
38. Railroad stop: abbr.
39. Horse's pace
40. Rock's Brian _____
41. Grand _____ Island
44. Japanese aborigine
45. Troubles, slangily
47. The ax, metaphorically
49. Low digits
50. German philosopher
51. Vienna's land
54. Game-show panelist Charles Nelson _____
58. "What's _____ for me?"
59. What did the rabbit say to the carrot? "It's been nice _____"
62. Carnival attraction
63. Maritime
64. Fish catcher
65. British gun
66. Keach of "Mike Hammer"
67. Demolition supplies

DOWN

1. Workout woe
2. "The Flim-_____ Man"
3. Tropical tuber
4. Purple birthstone
5. America's only marsupial
6. Bro, to sis
7. _____ polloi
8. Business letter abbr.
9. He played Gotti in "Gotti"
10. Is crazy about
11. What's the best way to send a letter to the Easter Bunny?
12. Words that precede "ever so humble"
13. Hullabaloos
18. Oboe piece
22. Wide ave.

24. Hard volleyball hit
25. Headstone inscription
27. Halley's _____
28. Clickable pictures
29. What side of a chicken has the most feathers?
31. "If I Had a Hammer" singer Lopez
32. Frame job
35. Mrs. Eisenhower
39. Old street fixture
41. Coffin support
42. Gives out, as homework

43. How a sore loser reacts
46. Corrupt
48. Sharp
51. Publicizes
52. The U in I.C.U.
53. Med. school subject
55. Rhone capital, to the French
56. Burglar's take
57. Some laughs
60. Gardner of "The Naked Maja"
61. WWII female

1	2	3	4		5	6	7	8	9		10	11	12	13
14					15						16			
17				18							19			
20							21		22					
			23			24	25		26					
27	28	29							30				31	32
33					34			35				36		
37						38					39			
40				41	42				43		44			
45			46				47			48				
		49				50								
51	52				53			54			55	56	57	
58				59		60	61							
62				63						64				
65				66						67				

Answers on page 179.

WORD LADDER

Change just one letter on each line to go from the top word to the bottom word. Do not change the order of the letters. You must have a common English word at each step.

RAINY

_____

_____

_____

_____

_____

WALKS

Answers on page 179.

PICTURE THIS

Place each of the 26 boxes in the 4 by 8 grid below so they form an Easter picture. Do this without cutting the page apart: Use only your eyes.

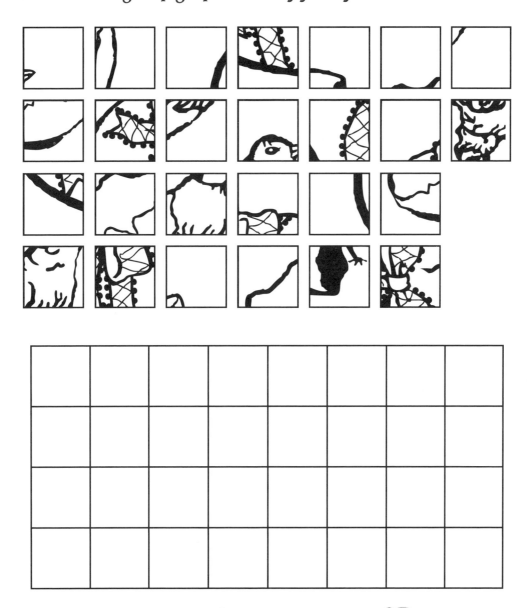

Answer on page 179.

WORD LADDER

Change just one letter on each line to go from the top word to the bottom word. Do not change the order of the letters. You must have a common English word at each step.

HOP

_____

_____

JOY

COMPLETE THE TALE

Below is a group of words that, when properly arranged in the blanks, reveal a quote from *The Tale of Peter Rabbit* by Beatrix Potter.

frightened   forgotten   gate   hands   thief

Mr. McGregor was on his ____ and knees planting out young cabbages, but he jumped up and ran after Peter, waving a rake and calling out, "Stop ____!" Peter was most dreadfully ____; he rushed all over the garden, for he had ____ the way back to the ____.

Answers on page 179.

SUDOKU

Use deductive logic to complete the grid so that each row, each column, and each 3 by 3 box contains the numbers 1 through 9 in some order. The solution is unique.

2	5		3	7	6	8		
						9		
8			1		5		3	
	9				3	1		
			8	6	9			
		2	4				9	
	4		5		7			6
		3						
		6	9	1	4		5	8

Answers on page 179.

EASTER FOOD

Every word listed is contained within the group of letters. Words can be found in a straight line horizontally, vertically, or diagonally. They may be read either forward or backward.

ASPARAGUS

BABKA

CABBAGE

CARROT CAKE

CHEESE

DOUGHNUTS

EGGS

FISH CAKES

HAM

LAMB

LEMON POTATOES

PASCUALINA

PICKLED HERRING

PIEROGI

PIZZELLE

PULLA

SPANAKOPITA

STUFFING

TORRIJAS

TZATZIKI

```
V N D C W T H Y E S E E H C A X
V K G A I I O A L L U P S I T S
N B N B I N X R U C E D G K I T
K I I B D R W F R I U A G I P U
J R R A H O G W G I T Y E Z O F
N N R G U C U O Q B J B V T K F
Z E E E K S R G K H M A L A A I
A L H Y X E O K H A U J S Z N N
U L D R I D A X L N V E I T A G
A E E P U V M I A S U D J L P N
T Z L E M O N P O T A T O E S L
B Z K A S P A R A G U S S O J Z
A I C A R R O T C A K E Q Z S X
B P I D T V V X U U I J M A H Z
K P P A S C U A L I N A N U R Z
A Q P V G P S E K A C H S I F H
```

Answers on page 179.

EASTER ANAGRAM

The following phrases are all anagrams for the same term related to Easter. What is it?

NEATEN SORBET

SONNETEER TAB

TORN ABSENTEE

M_SS_NG V_W_LS

Below is a quote from *The Adventures of Peter Cottontail* by Thornton W. Burgess. The only thing is, some terms have lost A, E, I, O, and U, as well as any punctuation and spaces between words. Can you figure out the missing vowels and decipher each term?

Jimmy was very PLT. He begged Reddy's PRDN. He protested that it was all a MSTK. He explained how Peter Rabbit had played a trick on both of them, and how he himself was just looking for beetles for BRKFST. Now, Reddy Fox is very quick tempered, and as soon as he realized that he had been made the VCTM of a joke, he lost his temper completely. He glared at Jimmy Skunk.

Answers on pages 179 & 180.

EASTER MAZE

Answer on page 180.

PIC-A-PIX

Use the clues on the left of every row and the top of every column to reveal the picture hidden in the grid below. Numbers indicate how many blocks get colored in, and the sequence in which they get colored. There must be at least one empty square between each sequence.

Column clues (read top to bottom; 25 columns):

1	2	3	4	5	6	7	8	9	10	11	12	13	14	15	16	17	18	19	20	21	22	23	24	25
								1	2															
							1	1	3															
					2	1	2	2	1	4					1	2	1							
				1	1	1	1	1	1	1	3			3	2	4	1	2			2			
		2	1	3	2	2	2	5	1	1	1	2	1	3	2	1	1	1	2	1		1		
	2	8	3	5	3	1	2	1	1	2	2	3	2	1	2	1	2	3	3	1	7	1		
	2	2	1	2	2	2	2	2	1	1	2	5	1	1	1	1	2	2	6	1	1	2	8	1
11	2	3	2	1	2	1	1	1	3	6	6	6	6	6	6	6	6	6	7	6	6	5	4	11

Row clues (top to bottom):

- 7
- 5 1 3
- 3 5 3
- 2 3 1 3 2
- 1 2 1 3 1 2 1
- 1 2 3 1 1 3 1
- 1 2 3 3 1
- 1 1 2 1
- 1 2 4 4 2 1
- 1 1 2 2 2 2 2 1
- 1 1 1 1 1 1 1 2 1
- 1 1 3 5 5 1
- 1 1 2 4 2 3 2 1
- 5 2 3 3 1 1
- 7 1 1 1 1 1 3
- 1 4 1 1 1 1 1 1 2 1
- 2 4 1 5 1
- 3 11 2
- 1 4 6
- 1 20
- 3 18
- 1 2 13
- 2 17
- 3 13
- 15

Answer on page 180.

EASTER IN GREECE (PART I)

Read the story below, then turn the page and answer the questions.

Red is a color usually associated with Christmas—candy canes, holly, the color of Santa Claus's coat—but for Greek Orthodox families, red is traditionally used at Easter time to dye their boiled eggs. The color red is meant to serve as religious representation: It symbolizes the blood of Jesus, as well as his victory over death. The hard shell of the egg represents the tomb of Christ. The eggs are dyed on Maundy Thursday, and on Easter Sunday each member of the family plays a game with the eggs, taking turns trying to crack them open by hitting them against one another. Whichever egg doesn't crack by the end of the game is declared the winner.

The Greek island of Corfu celebrates with another Easter tradition. In addition to dyeing red eggs, residents toss water-filled earthenware out of their windows and balconies beginning at 11 a.m. on Easter Saturday. Pots, pans, casserole dishes, flowerpots—anything clay or ceramic—are sent crashing down onto the street below. Special oversized pots are sometimes made specifically for the event.

The origin of the ritual is not known. Some people believe that the tradition was copied from the people of Venice, in Italy, who throw out their old possessions on New Year's Day. It could be that the tradition evolved to take place before Christ's rebirth instead. Others link the tradition to a sign of mourning: It creates a chaotic scene that mirrors the confusion and grief that took place after Jesus died on the cross. Mostly, however, people attribute it to the start of spring. The throwing of pots welcomes the season and symbolizes the new crops that are to be grown and gathered.

EASTER IN GREECE (PART II)

(Do not read this until you have read the previous page!)

1. According to the Greek Orthodox religion, what do the red hard-boiled eggs symbolize?
    - A. Jesus's victory over death
    - B. the blood of Jesus
    - C. the tomb of Jesus
    - D. all of the above

2. Traditionally, when are the red eggs dyed?
    - A. Maundy Thursday
    - B. Good Friday
    - C. Easter Saturday
    - D. Easter Sunday

3. What time do residents of Corfu begin throwing pots, pans, and flowerpots out their windows and balconies on Easter Saturday?
    - A. 9 a.m.
    - B. 10 a.m.
    - C. 11 a.m.
    - D. 12 p.m.

4. Some people attribute the tradition of tossing earthenware out the window to the similar Venetian tradition of throwing out old possessions on New Year's Eve.
    - _____ True
    - _____ False

Answers on page 180.

COMPLETE THE TALE

Below is a group of words that, when properly arranged in the blanks, reveal a quote from *The Tale of Peter Rabbit* by Beatrix Potter.

brass   cabbages   gooseberry   jacket   shoe

He lost one of his shoes among the ____, and the other ____ amongst the potatoes. After losing them, he ran on four legs and went faster, so that I think he might have got away altogether if he had not unfortunately run into a ____ net, and got caught by the large buttons on his ____. It was a blue jacket with ____ buttons, quite new.

Answers on page 180.

EASTER BASKET TREATS

Every word listed is contained within the group of letters. Words can be found in a straight line horizontally, vertically, or diagonally. They may be read either forward or backward.

BUBBLE WAND

CHOCOLATE BUNNY

COLORING BOOK

EASTER GRASS

ERASERS

GEL PENS

HOT WHEELS CARS

JELLY BEANS

JUMP ROPE

LEGOS

LIP BALM

MARBLES

NAIL POLISH

PENCILS

PEZ DISPENSERS

PLAY DOUGH

PLAYING CARDS

RIBBON

STICKERS

STUFFED ANIMAL

```
I P E N C I L S M T J L B C M C
Z P L A Y D O U G H U I U E A P
Z L Z H R I B B O N M P B R R P
X A I N O M W B F S P B B A B E
C Y N A U T X G W T R A L S L Z
O I L I S M W Q K U O L E E E D
L N B L T L V H Y F P M W R S I
O G V P I P I G E F E S A S U S
R C H O C O L A T E B U N N Y P
I A W L K B V I G D L V D R K E
N R K I E G R R N A L S T R X N
G D N S R J T W Q N E N C D U S
B S J H S J D M V I G T O A D E
O G E L P E N S N M O V X K R R
O E A S T E R G R A S S U H E S
K U Z B I W J E L L Y B E A N S
```

Answers on page 180.

MOST EXPENSIVE CHOCOLATE RABBIT

Cryptograms are messages in substitution code. Break the code to read the message. For example, THE SMART CAT might become FVO QWGDF JGF if **F** is substituted for **T**, **V** for **H**, **O** for **E**, and so on.

Xkzxzyqrcwep xzjw tn gcrk wyqizeqrw wuciyw xewqrczmp rkeztfkztr rkw awqe, qmu Wqprwe cp mz whxwnrczm. Cm 2015, gzeyu-ewmzgmwu xzmswxrczmwe qmu szejwe xkws zs Kqeezup, Jqercm Xkcsswep, gzelwu cm xzyyqizeqrczm gcrk rkw xzjnqma 77 Ucqjzmup rz xewqrw rkw gzeyu'p jzpr whreqdqfqmr xkzxzyqrw Wqprwe itmma. Xkcsswep pnwmr rgz-qmu-q-kqys 16-kzte uqap xqewstyya rwjnwecmf, izmucmf, qmu xqedcmf 75% pcmfyw zecfcm Rqmbqmcqm xkzxzyqrw cmrz rkw pkqnw zs q eqiicr 1 szzr, 3 cmxkwp rqyy. Crp wawp gwew cmyqcu gcrk rgz pkcmcmf ucqjzmup. Rkeww pzycu xkzxzyqrw wffp xzdwewu cm fzyu ywqs pqr qr crp iqpw. Rkw xkzxzyqrw eqiicr kqu qnnezhcjqrwya 548,000 xqyzecwp—itr gcrk qm wotqyya kwsra necxw rqf zs $63,000, azt gztyum'r iw rzz rwjnrwu rz rqlw q icrw.

Answers on page 180.

COMPLETE THE TALE

Below is a group of words that, when properly arranged in the blanks, reveal a quote from *The Tale of Peter Rabbit* by Beatrix Potter.

exert   shed   sieve   sparrows   water

Peter gave himself up for lost, and ____ big tears; but his sobs were overheard by some friendly ____, who flew to him in great excitement, and implored him to ____ himself. Mr. McGregor came up with a ____, which he intended to pop upon the top of Peter; but Peter wriggled out just in time, leaving his jacket behind him. And rushed into the tool-shed, and jumped into a can. It would have been a beautiful thing to hide in, if it had not had so much ____ in it.

Answers on page 180.

LARGEST CHOCOLATE RABBIT

Cryptograms are messages in substitution code. Break the code to read the message. For example, THE SMART CAT might become FVO QWGDF JGF if **F** is substituted for **T**, **V** for **H**, **O** for **E**, and so on.

Nejwmbkw cmj rbljd nh jnee nh jwd tmuez'h
enukdhj vwmvmenjd dkk, jwd tmuez'h enukdhj
unaalj fnzd sumf vwmvmenjd tnh hjlee n hlkwj
jm adwmez! Vudnjdz mc Sdaubnuq 25, 2017, aq
Drblod zn Vnhn zm Vwmvmenjd nj Hwmoolck
Badunan lc Badunan, Flcnh Kdunlh, Aungle, jwd
knukncjbnc abccq tdlkwdz 9359.7 ombczh. Lj
fdnhbudz nooumylfnjdeq 14 sddj, 8 lcvwdh jnee;
wnz n tlzjw ms 6 sddj, 9 lcvwdh nj ljh tlzdhj
omlcj; ncz tnh cdnueq 5 sddj, 8 lcvwdh emck.
N jmjne ms 9 vwmvmenjldulck oumsdhhlmcneh
tmuxdz mpdu 8 vmchdvbjlpd znqh jm vudnjd jwd
unaalj hvbeojbud. Jwd oudplmbh wmezdu ms jwd
udvmuz, Zbunvdee Hmbjw Nsulvn lc Fnuvw 2010,
vudnjdz n abccq jwnj fdnhbudz nooumylfnjdeq
12 sddj jnee.

BARROW OF FLOWERS

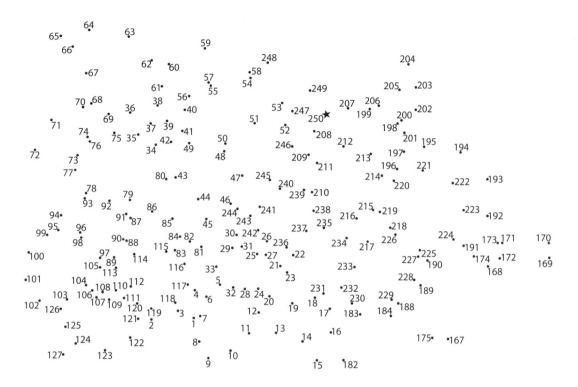

Answer on page 181.

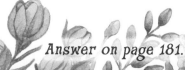

WORD LADDER

Change just one letter on each line to go from the top word to the bottom word. Do not change the order of the letters. You must have a common English word at each step.

ROSE

____

____

____

____

____

BUDS

Answers on page 181.

EASTER IN GUATEMALA (PART I)

Read the story below, then turn the page and answer the questions.

Every morning of Holy Week, or *Semana Santa*, locals of Antigua, Guatemala, fill the cobblestone streets holding baskets of flower petals, palm leaves, and dyed sawdust. These materials are used to create elaborate carpets, or *alfombras*, that transform the city block into a bright and colorful display. According to *Smithsonian Magazine*, once these sawdust carpets are complete, thousands of people will join daily processions walking over them, "typically beginning inside one of the local churches [...] and then travers[ing] through different neighborhoods."

The creation of one of these colorful carpets is quite labor-intensive. First, sand or undyed sawdust is used to fill in any gaps in the cobblestone streets and to make the ground level. Wooden planks are placed down on the ground as a form of scaffolding, and artists balance on them so as not to disturb their carpet creations. To create smaller, more intricate details, cardboard stencils are sometimes used. Each carpet displays a different scene. Some are religious, depicting Christian imagery of Jesus on the cross, while others highlight the beauty of the natural world: colorful flowers, leaves, and birds. Still others represent Mayan traditions of Guatemalan history—you don't have to be Catholic to get involved in the art.

Due to the amount of labor required, the carpets are often finished mere moments before crowds of people step foot on them. After the procession is complete, dump trucks and sweepers clean up whatever remains and recycle it into compost. Then, preparations for the next day of sawdust alfombras begin.

EASTER IN GUATEMALA (PART II)

(Do not read this until you have read the previous page!)

1. Which of the following materials is NOT used to make Guatemala's colorful carpets?
   A. colored sand
   B. dyed sawdust
   C. flower petals
   D. palm leaves

2. Which of the following materials is used to help make cobblestone streets level?
   A. gravel
   B. mud
   C. uncooked rice
   D. undyed sawdust

3. Artists balance on woven mats so as not to disturb their carpet creations.
   _____ True
   _____ False

4. After the procession is over, dump trucks clean up whatever remains and dispose of it in a landfill.
   _____ True
   _____ False

Answers on page 181.

EASTER MAZE

Answer on page 181.

THINGS FOUND IN EASTER EGGS

Every word listed is contained within the group of letters. Words can be found in a straight line horizontally, vertically, or diagonally. They may be read either forward or backward.

BALLOONS	ERASERS
BOUNCY BALLS	GUM
BRACELET	GUMMY BEARS
BUBBLES	JELLY BEANS
CASH	LICORICE
CHALK	NAIL POLISH
CHAPSTICK	PRETZELS
CHOCOLATE	RAISINS
COINS	RING
CRAYONS	STICKERS

```
K C A C N S U S R A I S I N S S
S O C G P D S R E S A R E C X P
R I T S M G A C C R A Y O N S X
E N L I B O U N V L T I A X C R
K S I B M B A L L O O N S Q W S
C H C K O X S E L B B U B W V R
I K O W G U M M Y B E A R S B V
T H R O G V N A I L P O L I S H
S R I O N B U C H O C O L A T E
H W C A I K Z Z Y F L O J G M O
B U E M R G R E U B E R X K J L
B R A C E L E T C H A L K Q G P
H S A C S N A E B Y L L E J C H
H O K C I T S P A H C G L E K Z
R M O T V C F D P C C B S S C M
B Y Q A E S L E Z T E R P G U M
```

Answers on page 181.

M_SS_NG V_W_LS

Below is a quote from *The Adventures of Peter Cottontail* by Thornton W. Burgess. The only thing is, some terms have lost A, E, I, O, and U, as well as any punctuation and spaces between words. Can you figure out the missing vowels and decipher each term?

Old Granny Fox was not feeling well. For three days she had been unable to go out HNTNG, and for three days Reddy Fox had tried to find something to tempt Granny's PPTT. He had brought in a tender young CHCKN from Farmer Brown's hen yard, and he had stolen a plump TRT from Billy Mink's storehouse, but Granny had just turned up her nose. "What I need," said Granny Fox, "is a tender young RBBT."

CANDY ADDAGRAM

This puzzle functions exactly like an anagram with an added step: In addition to being scrambled, each term below is missing the same letter. Discover the missing letter, then unscramble the words. When you do, you'll reveal 5 terms associated with Easter candy.

ACCESS REPERTOIRES (three words)

BLANDLY THIN COCONUT (three words)

CUMBERED CRAGGY (three words)

MALAPROP WHELMS (two words)

WRONG BIG SHOPPERS (three words)

 Answers on pages 181 & 182.

LARGEST RABBIT

Cryptograms are messages in substitution code. Break the code to read the message. For example, THE SMART CAT might become FVO QWGDF JGF if **F** is substituted for **T**, **V** for **H**, **O** for **E**, and so on.

Haoqcmz Ucbxi sbjjcim bso izo absuomi jsoov dh vdqomicw sbjjci bxv, zcmidscwbaak, noso lori bm b eicacik jsoov hds izocs hes bxv qobi. Jowbemo dh izocs vdwcao bxv rbicoxi xbieso, idvbk izok bso dhiox lori bm roim. Izomo uoxiao ucbxim ikrcwbaak nocuz joinoox 15 id 20 rdexvm, sobwzcxu aoxuizm dh bjdei 2.5 id 4 hooi nzox heaak misoiwzov dei. Dxo Haoqcmz ucbxi sbjjci, zdnofos, moi b xon sowdsv hds cim mrowcom: Vbscem, dnxov jk Bxxoiio Ovnbsvm cx izo Exciov Lcxuvdq, nbm hdexv id nocuz 49 rdexvm bxv qobmesov b heaa 4 hooi, 3 cxwzom adxu.

Answers on page 182.

EGG-CELLENT

Every word or phrase listed is contained within the box of letters below. The words can be found in a straight line horizontally, vertically, or diagonally. They may read either forward or backward. The leftover letters will reveal three more egg-y phrases.

ARPEGGIO

BARE-LEGGED

BEGGAR

BOOTLEGGER

EGGDROP SOUP

EGGHEAD

EGG MCMUFFIN

EGGROLL

GREGG

KEGGER

L'EGGO MY EGGO

LEGGY

PEGGY LEE

POACHED EGGS

REGGAE

REGGIE BAR

VEGGIES

Leftover letters:

_____

```
E K D E G G E L E R A B
G G E S E E L Y G G E P
B L E G G O M Y E G G O
S E I G G E V E G O N A
R E G G I E B A R I E C
P U O S P O R D G G E H
D N I F F U M C M G G E
I B O O T L E G G E R D
C T H A M A E H N P E E
L L O R G G E G D R G G
E R E G G A E G G A G G
G S E G D G Y O L Y K S
```

Answers on page 182.

EASTER EQUALS

Americans sure love their Easter celebrations! Below are several U.S.-based statistics revolving around the Easter holiday. Match each figure to its correct number.

1. Chocolate bunnies consumed each Easter

2. Dollar price of the world's most expensive chocolate bunny

3. Dollars spent on Easter candy each year

4. Egg-dying kits sold annually

5. Eggs decorated each Easter

6. Jelly beans consumed each Easter

7. Marshmallow Peeps consumed each Easter

8. Wooden eggs made for the annual White House Easter Egg Roll

A. 49,000

B. 80,000

C. 16 million

D. 90 million

E. 180 million

F. 1.5 billion

G. 3.1 billion

H. 16 billion

Answers on page 182.

FLOWERS & BOOTS

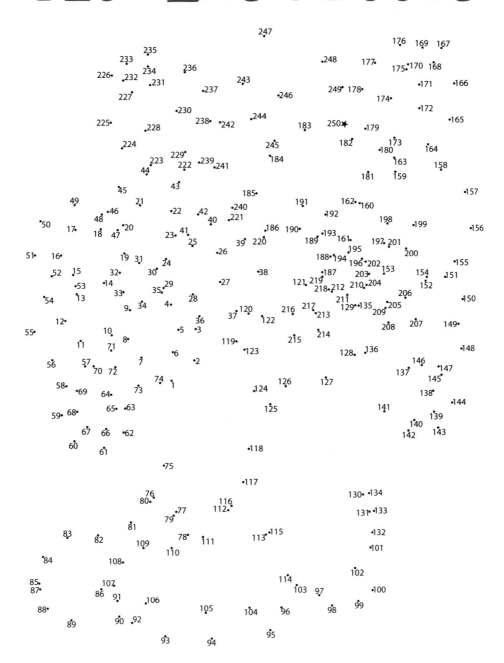

Answer on page 182.

WORD LADDER

Change just one letter on each line to go from the top word to the bottom word. Do not change the order of the letters. You must have a common English word at each step.

CANDY

_____

_____

_____

_____

_____

PEEPS

 Answers on page 182.

BROKEN EGG

What letter was painted on this egg before it was broken?

Answer on page 182.

PICTURE THIS

Place each of the 25 boxes in the 6 by 5 grid below so they form an Easter picture. Do this without cutting the page apart: Use only your eyes.

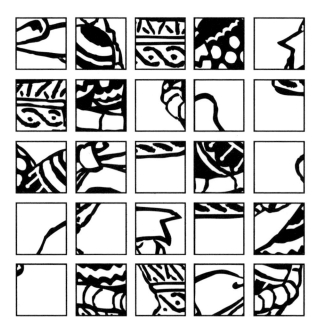
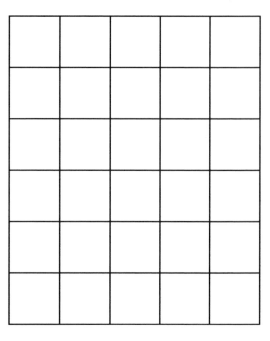

Answer on page 182.

EARLIEST HOLLOW CHOCOLATE EGG

Cryptograms are messages in substitution code. Break the code to read the message. For example, THE SMART CAT might become FVO QWGDF JGF if F is substituted for T, V for H, O for E, and so on.

Htrdzde xu azxowy pue spyydzude btxc pue sphmde xuyt p ati, hwthtcpyd Dpnydz doon fxowy nddf cxmd p szdyyg zdhduy xurduyxtu— aky ywxum popxu! Ywd dpzcxdny wtcctq hwthtcpyd doon qdzd sztekhde xu ywd Kuxyde Mxuoetf ag Bzg'n, p bpfxcg-tqude htfspug, aphm xu 1873. Bzpuhd pue Odzfpug wpe ntce ntcxe hwthtcpyd doon btz ntfd yxfd adbtzd, aky xy qpnu'y kuyxc Bzg'n bxokzde tky wtq yt ndspzpyd hthtp akyydz bztf ywd hthtp adpu ywpy ywd udq, wtcctq edcxhphg yttm tbb. Bzg'n htfsdyxytzn vkxhmcg hpkowy tu yt ywd yzdue pue, yqt gdpzn cpydz, ywd bxzny Hpeakzg Dpnydz Doon qdzd hzdpyde.

BREAK TIME

ACROSS

1. Boaters and beanies
5. Tote
8. AFL partner, once
11. Blunted sword
12. Arg. neighbor
13. Like "California Girls," key-wise
14. Change in Rome, once
15. Get the last bit of suds out
17. Moveable feast with many eggs
19. L.A.-to-Las Vegas dir.
20. Elsie's sound
21. "Well done!" in Italy
22. "___ for Noose" (Grafton book)
23. Did some rowing
24. Gambol playfully
27. Days of yore, quaintly
28. Asian nanny
29. Coaching legend Parseghian
30. Little bit of gel
33. Declaration day
36. Like a secure professor
37. Brief bio, in passing
38. "Dancing With the Stars" network
39. Dubai's country: abbr.
40. Okeechobee, for one
41. Slangy refusal
42. Publisher's staff, for short
43. Gifts in long boxes

DOWN

1. Troy beauty
2. Bee-related
3. Using few words
4. Sofa or bench
5. Grand Canyon critters
6. "You ___ Beautiful" (Joe Cocker hit)
7. Hindu spiritual guide
8. Hot coal
9. Bonkers
10. Did as told
16. ___ with (not favored by)
18. Kuwaiti leader
22. India's first P. M.
23. Name of five Norwegian kings
24. Lounging garment
25. One-celled organism
26. Pot belly

27. Eats away at

29. Get ___ (succeed)

30. Home of Emirates Airline

31. How great minds think

32. Eight-bit groups

34. Steadfast

35. Rough blow

1	2	3	4		5	6	7		8	9	10
11					12				13		
14					15		16				
17				18							
19				20				21			
			22				23				
24	25	26				27					
28					29				30	31	32
33				34				35			
36								37			
38				39				40			
41				42				43			

Answers on page 183.

PIC-A-PIX

Use the clues on the left of every row and the top of every column to reveal the picture hidden in the grid below. Numbers indicate how many blocks get colored in, and the sequence in which they get colored. There must be at least one empty square between each sequence.

Column clues (left to right, read top to bottom):

Column	Clue
1	8 5
2	2 1 2 1 2
3	2 2 2 1 1 1
4	1 5 1 1
5	2 2 3 2 1 1 1
6	1 1 1 1 1 2 1 1
7	1 3 4 3 1
8	1 2 1 1
9	1 1 1 2 6
10	1 1 1 2
11	2 1 1 1 7 1
12	1 3 2 2 2
13	1 1 1 2 4 1
14	1 2 3 2 1 2
15	2 2 1 1 1 1 1 1
16	2 3 2 1 3
17	6 1 1 1 1 1
18	1 1 1 3
19	2 1 2
20	4

Row clues (top to bottom):

Row	Clue
1	3 5
2	3 4 2
3	2 1 2 2
4	2 3 1 1 1
5	1 2 1 1 2 2 1
6	1 1 1 1 1 1
7	1 2 2 1 1
8	1 2 1 1 1 2
9	1 3 1 2 4
10	1 1 4 2 2
11	2 6 1 1
12	3 1 1 1 1
13	3 1 6
14	2 1 1 1
15	2 2 1 1 1 1 1 2
16	1 1 2 1 1 2 1 1 1
17	2 1 1 1 1 1
18	1 1 5 1 6
19	2 2 1 1 1 2
20	10 1 4

Answer on page 183.

EASTER ANAGRAM

The following phrases are all anagrams for the same term related to Easter. What is it?

BAN YE JELL

BY JANELLE

JAY BELL EN

M_SS_NG V_W_LS

Below is a quote from *The Adventures of Peter Cottontail* by Thornton W. Burgess. The only thing is, some terms have lost A, E, I, O, and U, as well as any punctuation and spaces between words. Can you figure out the missing vowels and decipher each term?

Peter Rabbit crept out of his snug little bed in the MDDL of the Old Briar-patch two hours before sun-up and HRRD over to the big hickory-tree. Sure enough, close by, he found a beautiful bed of sweet CLVR, just as Reddy Fox had said was there. Peter CHCKLD to himself as he ate and ate and ate, until his little round STMCH was so full that he could hardly hop.

Answers on page 183.

JELLY BEAN FLAVORS

Every word listed is contained within the group of letters. Words can be found in a straight line horizontally, vertically, or diagonally. They may be read either forward or backward.

A&W CREAM SODA	COTTON CANDY
A&W ROOT BEER	CRUSHED PINEAPPLE
BERRY BLUE	DR PEPPER
BLUEBERRY	FRENCH VANILLA
BUBBLE GUM	GREEN APPLE
BUTTERED POPCORN	ISLAND PUNCH
CANTALOUPE	JUICY PEAR
CAPPUCCINO	KIWI
CARAMEL CORN	LEMON DROP
CHILI MANGO	LEMON LIME
CHOCOLATE PUDDING	LICORICE
CINNAMON	MANGO
COCONUT	

```
W B O X Q T M D R P E P P E R A S K Y E C I
L F X W N T T N L I C O R I C E K W V K O R
E K R P K G H A M M I S U W T M O T Y C T U
F M I S L A N D P U N C H R S U D Z G V T Y
G C A R A M E L C O R N J J U K L X I Y O D
R A W R O O T B E E R R C Y J U Z W H O N E
E P W L B U T T E R E D P O P C O R N V C T
E P J C T D A C H R C I N N A M O N S M A N
N U M A R L A M A K R H E O W X Q S X R N Z
A C R N R E F X K J S Y I W C G S R M G D Y
P C Z T J T A U L P E O B L U E B E R R Y I
P I D A F A E M S Y W O U L I N J K S M E U
L N O L B V M V S E H U B D U M F Z A K Q W
E O C O C O N U T O U S B M E E A I R I E U
T N F U N T T C G Q D Q L N G F E N Z W U J
A U Q P Q X V G P O Y A E G J E Q W G I Y H
M X X E K W Y M Y W P F G T T Q X D Q O J I
E X C H O C O L A T E P U D D I N G T J N Y
S V O L E M O N D R O P M L E M O N L I M E
Q V B P B K X H J U I C Y P E A R M A N G O
F R E N C H V A N I L L A Q S N D P T D J M
Y M K Y C R U S H E D P I N E A P P L E U K
```

Answers on page 183.

SUDOKU

Use deductive logic to complete the grid so that each row, each column, and each 3 by 3 box contains the numbers 1 through 9 in some order. The solution is unique.

8	1	2		7				
5			3					
9				2		6		
	8		9	4				
4		3	1		6	8		2
				3	2		5	
		6		1				3
					5			4
				6		5	8	7

Answers on page 183.

COMPLETE THE TALE

Below is a group of words that, when properly arranged in the blanks, reveal a quote from *The Tale of Peter Rabbit* by Beatrix Potter.

carefully   flower-pot   sneezed   tool-shed   tried

Mr. McGregor was quite sure that Peter was somewhere in the ____, perhaps hidden underneath a ____. He began to turn them over ____, looking under each. Presently Peter ____–"Kertyschoo!" Mr. McGregor was after him in no time. And ____ to put his foot upon Peter, who jumped out of a window, upsetting three plants.

Answers on page 183.

EASTER MAZE

Answer on page 184.

EASTER IN HUNGARY (PART I)

Read the story below, then turn the page and answer the questions.

Like other countries in Central and Eastern Europe, Hungary's Easter Monday traditions have long revolved around soaking young women with copious amounts of water. It's a cleansing ritual dating back to pre-Christian symbols of fertility, and meant to preserve the youth and beauty of the girls drenched. It would have been a common sight to see boys chasing after girls with buckets of water—until recently. Now the tradition of *locsolkodás*, or sprinkling, has taken on a new look.

The more gentle form of locsolkodás involves, not water, but perfume or cologne. Young men spray or sprinkle drops of the sweet aroma onto the girl's hair or neck. As they do so, they recite a locsoló verse, a kind of short poem that asks the girls for permission to sprinkle them. These can range from nursery rhymes to more humorous poems with racy elements.

As a reward for their performance, the boys receive a gift, usually a painted egg. Much like how water or perfume symbolizes purification, the egg is a symbol for rebirth, fertility, and new life. Other gifts might include chocolate, a homemade dessert, coins—or even a small shot of alcohol. It may seem like an unfair exchange at first, but it's all done tongue-in-cheek.

EASTER IN HUNGARY (PART II)

(Do not read this until you have read the previous page!)

1. Which qualities of a woman does the tradition of locsolkodás aim to preserve?
   A. her kindness and compassion
   B. her talent and skill
   C. her wisdom and knowledge
   D. her youth and beauty

2. What is the intended purpose of the locsoló poem?
   A. to ask girls for permission to sprinkle them
   B. to demand girls hand over a painted egg
   C. to impress girls with outstanding storytelling talents
   D. to remind girls of their youth and beauty

3. In Hungary, the egg is a symbol for rebirth, fertility, and new life.
   _____ True
   _____ False

4. In addition to the painted egg, what is another example of a possible gift?
   A. an apple
   B. coins
   C. flowers
   D. a handkerchief

Answers on page 184.

COMPLETE THE TALE

Below is a group of words that, when properly arranged in the blanks, reveal a quote from *The Tale of Peter Rabbit* by Beatrix Potter.

can   idea   running   trembling   window

The ____ was too small for Mr. McGregor, and he was tired of ____ after Peter. He went back to his work. Peter sat down to rest; he was out of breath and ____ with fright, and he had not the least ____ which way to go. Also he was very damp with sitting in that ____. After a time he began to wander about, going lippity–lippity–not very fast, and looking all round.

Answers on page 184.

MORE JELLY BEAN FLAVORS

Every word listed is contained within the group of letters. Words can be found in a straight line horizontally, vertically, or diagonally. They may be read either forward or backward.

MARGARITA

MIXED BERRY SMOOTHIE

ORANGE SHERBET

PEACH

PIÑA COLADA

PLUM

POMEGRANATE

RASPBERRY

RED APPLE

SIZZLING CINNAMON

SOUR CHERRY

STRAWBERRY CHEESE-CAKE

STRAWBERRY DAIQUIRI

STRAWBERRY JAM

SUNKIST LEMON

SUNKIST LIME

SUNKIST ORANGE

SUNKIST PINK GRAPEFRUIT

SUNKIST TANGERINE

TOASTED MARSHMALLOW

TOP BANANA

TUTTI-FRUTTI

VERY CHERRY

WATERMELON

WILD BLACKBERRY

```
G T O A S T E D M A R S H M A L L O W B G X
P Q R J M T K Q S U N K I S T O R A N G E S
S K A O R I R D G E X H F T P E A C H E O I
U S N D L E X P R R T F X R I A R P G F R Z
N O G O M R D E I T O P B A N A N A S H A Z
K U E P S K Y A D J S B B W F V H M V O S L
I R S I U Z W C P B R D Y B T J Z P F R P I
S C H N N U A J R P E D A E I N V L N B B N
T H E A K A T K L H L R A R N R E T G A E G
L E R C I V E R Y C H E R R Y L K H P R C
I R B O S T R A W B E R R Y D A I Q U I R I
M R E L T X M P Z L X L J C S F Z L T J Y N
E Y T A T G E T L Z M M K H W M K V S S R N
V F K D A S L J B U O M N E M B O L A L F A
S C I A N N O P A H M B Y E D A D O N O G M
Q T H P G P N O E Z L N N S X M W O T Q Z O
S P O M E G R A N A T E Q E X Z M L L H L N
H F B W R F W I L D B L A C K B E R R Y I N
S U N K I S T P I N K G R A P E F R U I T E
K V U J N S H B F B S U N K I S T L E M O N
I V X I E Z N S T R A W B E R R Y J A M Z C
K B T U T T I F R U T T I M A R G A R I T A
```

Answers on page 184.

BLOOM WHERE YOU'RE PLANTED

Answer on page 184.

EASTER ANAGRAM

The following phrases are all anagrams for the same term related to Easter. What is it?

ALLEY TIRES

EARLY ISLET

LAYER TILES

COMPLETE THE TALE

Below is a group of words that, when properly arranged in the blanks, reveal a quote from *The Tale of Peter Rabbit* by Beatrix Potter.

answer   door   gate   stone   wood

He found a _____ in a wall; but it was locked, and there was no room for a fat little rabbit to squeeze underneath. An old mouse was running in and out over the _____ doorstep, carrying peas and beans to her family in the _____. Peter asked her the way to the _____, but she had such a large pea in her mouth that she could not _____. She only shook her head at him. Peter began to cry.

Answers on page 184.

LONGEST LINE OF CHOCOLATE EGGS

Cryptograms are messages in substitution code. Break the code to read the message. For example, THE SMART CAT might become FVO QWGDF JGF if F is substituted for T, V for H, O for E, and so on.

Bam cxshv smrxsv gxs bam hxoymnb heom xg raxrxhtbm myyn ctn traempmv xo Tqseh 16, 2017, ld Ntobxna Neoya Stctb tov aen bthmobmv bmtj tb bam ZC Jtssexbb Jfjlte Ntats eo Jfjlte, Eovet. Thbaxfya bam 20,203 raxrxhtbm myyn jeyab oxb atpm lmmo rxonevmsmv oxbmcxsbad eovepevfthhd, qfb bxymbams bamd jmtnfsmv t bxbth venbtorm xg 1026 jmbmsn, xs 3366.14 gmmb. Gxhhxceoy bam rxorhfnexo xg bam smrxsv tbbmjqb, bam raxrxhtbm myyn cmsm venqhtdmv gxs nthm.

WORD LADDER

Change just one letter on each line to go from the top word to the bottom word. Do not change the order of the letters. You must have a common English word at each step.

GREEN

_____

_____ (very wooded)

_____

_____ (long lock of hair)

_____

_____

GRASS

 Answers on page 184.

FAMOUS BUNNIES

Think you know your renowned rabbits? Find these fictional furry critters in the grid. Words can be found in a straight line horizontally, vertically, or diagonally. They may read either forward or backward.

BABS BUNNY
(TINY TOON ADVENTURES)

BIGWIG (WATERSHIP DOWN)

BUGS BUNNY (LOONY TUNES)

BUSTER BUNNY
(TINY TOON ADVENTURES)

CADBURY BUNNY
(TV COMMERCIAL)

CAPTAIN CARROT
(DC COMICS)

DANDELION
(WATERSHIP DOWN)

EASTER BUNNY

ENERGIZER BUNNY
(TV COMMERCIAL)

FIVER (WATERSHIP DOWN)

HARE
(THE TORTOISE AND THE HARE)

HARVEY (HARVEY)

HODGE-PODGE
(BLOOM COUNTY)

LITTLE BUNNY FOO FOO
(NURSERY RHYME)

MARCH HARE
(ALICE IN WONDERLAND)

NESQUIK RABBIT
(TV COMMERCIAL)

PAT THE BUNNY
(PAT THE BUNNY)

PEEPS (MARSHMALLOW BUNNIES)

PETER COTTONTAIL
(HERE COMES PETER COTTONTAIL)

PETER RABBIT
(THE TALE OF PETER RABBIT)

RABBIT (WINNIE THE POOH)

RICOCHET RABBIT (MAGILLA GORILLA)

ROGER RABBIT
(WHO FRAMED ROGER RABBIT?)

THUMPER (BAMBI)

TRIX RABBIT (TV COMMERCIAL)

VELVETEEN RABBIT
(THE VELVETEEN RABBIT)

WHITE RABBIT
(ALICE IN WONDERLAND)

```
N A B R O Y N N U B R E Z I G R E N E U
E T N I B I C N P E T E R R A B B I T E
S T Y C U E A S T E R B U N N Y M I L L
Q T T O S I P O N T I B B A R R E G O R
U I I C T C T I B B A R E T I H W O H O
I B B H E L A C O L A R E T E B F N U N
K B B E R T I B B A R R E R B O N O I E
R A A T B S N A A R A E M V O A B I D Y
A R R R U E C F T H A R E F I I O L R N
B N X A N E A A H N A S Y T G F E E R N
B E I B N E R C A B O N C W H Y E D A U
I E R B Y R R B B B N T I U T W R N H B
T T T I I A O I A U U G T C H E P A A E
R E T T M D T O B P E G D O P E G D O H
E V O P L H E E S E A T S M C F I R S T
T L A M A A L P B Z I N U B G R L Y S T
E E V R E T E N U T Y H S I U X E P E A
R V V C T E E N N T T O F P E N O T P P
L E E I P S T A N R T W I T H T N H E E
Y E L Y N N U B Y R U B D A C A R Y S P
```

Answers on page 185.

M_SS_NG V_W_LS

Below is a quote from *The Adventures of Peter Cottontail* by Thornton W. Burgess. The only thing is, some terms have lost A, E, I, O, and U, as well as any punctuation and spaces between words. Can you figure out the missing vowels and decipher each term?

He made three long hops STRGHT towards Reddy Fox, all the time keeping the old STRWHT over him. Of course the hat went along with him, and, because it CVRD Peter all up, it looked for all the world as if the hat was alive. Reddy Fox gave one more long look at the STRNG thing coming towards him through the CBBG bed, and then he started for home as fast as he could go, his tail between his legs.

CLEANING ADDAGRAM

This puzzle functions exactly like an anagram with an added step: In addition to being scrambled, each term below is missing the same letter. Discover the missing letter, then unscramble the words. When you do, you'll reveal 5 terms associated with spring cleaning.

CITRUS BELT (two words)

CLEAVE PENNED (three words)

LINE SIGH (two words)

REALIZING WAVERERS (two words)

ROUGH SPASM (two words)

 Answers on page 185.

EASTER IN MEXICO (PART I)

Read the story below, then turn the page and answer the questions.

Some Easter traditions are more intense than others. Take, for instance, the Mexican Easter custom known as the Burning of the Judas. It takes place on Holy Saturday, the day before Easter—the same day the disciple Judas Iscariot who infamously betrayed Jesus to Roman authorities for money is thought to have died. The tradition involves stringing up an effigy representing Judas in public spaces, and destroying it with fire and explosives. The Burning of Judas was once widely practiced across the European Christian world; Austria, Czech Republic, England, Germany, Greece, Portugal, and Spain—to name a few—all participated in the folk tradition. It is thought that the Spanish took this tradition with them to Mexico in the New World.

Mexico made a few changes, however. Firstly, they replaced the crude human figure with hard papier-mâché artistic renderings, a style called *cartoneria*. Then, they focused on the custom's symbolism. Because of Judas' unspeakable sin of betraying the son of God, the apostle has long since been considered an icon of evil and corruption in the Catholic faith. But, according to Mexico, evil and corruption can take many forms. In recent years, crowds celebrating the Burning of Judas have used the effigies to instead represent dishonest public figures like politicians and businessmen.

It was this version of the tradition that nearly wiped out the entire ritual: Those in power decided to ban the practice at various points during the country's history. Today, however, the tradition has come back in full force. Although special permits are required to burn the effigy, the custom has cemented itself as an integral part of Mexico's Easter celebration.

EASTER IN MEXICO (PART II)

(Do not read this until you have read the previous page!)

1. The Mexican tradition of the Burning of Judas takes place on Maundy Thursday—the same day the disciple Judas Iscariot infamously betrayed Jesus to Roman authorities for money.
   _____ True
   _____ False

2. Which country is thought to have taken this tradition from Europe to Mexico in the New World?
   A. France
   B. Italy
   C. Portugal
   D. Spain

3. What does *cartoneria* refer to?
   A. clay human figures
   B. explosive pyrotechnics
   C. papier-mâché sculptures
   D. strung-up effigies

4. Today, special permits are required in order to burn the Easter effigy.
   _____ True
   _____ False

MOST ENTRANTS IN AN EGG HUNT

Cryptograms are messages in substitution code. Break the code to read the message. For example, THE SMART CAT might become FVO QWGDF JGF if **F** is substituted for **T**, **V** for **H**, **O** for **E**, and so on.

Hfm tgih mrhxkrhi wr kr mzz fnrh sgtamhwhwgr oki ksfwmqml yd hfm Bkymxzm Ywz Mzz Fnrh, ofwsf oki k 2012 sfkxwhd bnrlxkwiwrz sktakwzr iagrigxml yd hfm umomcmx Bkymxzm. Kaaxgvwtkhmcd 200 kxhwihi, smcmyxwhwmi, krl lmiwzrmxi omxm sgttwiiwgrml hg sxmkhm krl akwrh ckxzm bwymxzckii mzzi, ofwsf omxm hfmr acksml wr imcmshml cgskhwgri hfxgnzfgnh Cgrlgr. Ymzwrrwrz Bmyxnkxd 21, 12,773 akxhwswakrhi fkl 40 lkdi hg cgskhm hfm qkxwgni zwkrh mzzi cgskhml kxgnrl hfm skawhkc. Kssgxlwrz hg Bkymxzm'i omyiwhm, hfm owrrmx gb hfm mzz fnrh—ofg sfgim hg xmtkwr krgrdtgni—oki zwqmr hfm Unywcmm Mzz Axwjm: k xgim zgcl, lwktgrl, krl axmswgni ihgrm Bkymxzm mzz ogxhf £100,000. Hfm Ywz Mzz Fnrh xkwiml gqmx £1 twccwgr bgx hog sfkxwhwmi—krl imh k ogxcl xmsgxl wr hfm axgsmii!

Answers on page 185.

EASTER MAZE

Answer on page 185.

146• 145•
170★ 144
147• 169• 143
148• 168• 142
167•
149• 166•
150• 165•
151• 164•
163•
152• 155
153• 102
154★ 103
105• 104
106•
107•
108• 92•
109• 91•
110• 111•
89★ 112
88•
87• 23• 22•
86• 24•
85• 26•
84•
83•
82•
81•
80•
79•
78•
77•
201★ 76•
200•
75•
199•
198• 196•
197•
72•
71•
70
132• 131•
133• 130•
134• 129•
135• 162★ 128•
141• 161• 127•
140• 136• 126•
137• 159•
139• 160•
138• 125•
156 157 158★ 124•
123•
95•
96• 122•
97★ 121•
98• 120•
99• 119•
100•
101★ 118• •171
116 117 •172
1•
19 2•
21 3• 34•
20 •173
18★ •174
17• 4•
16• 5• 35• •175
15• 6• •176
14• 7• 36• •182
13• 8• •183
12• 9• 37• 177• •184
11• 10★ 38• 178• •185
59• 39• 179• •186
60• 57• 40• 180• •187
33 58• 41•
61• 56• 42•★ •188
62• 55• 181• 189•
63• 194 54• 43• •190
64★ 193 44•
195 53• •191
65• 52• 45•★192
66• 51• 46•
67• 50• 47•
68• 49• 48•
69
90• 113 115
114 93 94

Answer on page 185.

BUNNY BREEDS

Every word listed is contained within the group of letters. Words can be found in a straight line horizontally, vertically, or diagonally. They may be read either forward or backward.

AMERICAN SABLE	HARLEQUIN
ANGORA	HAVANA
BELGIAN HARE	HIMALAYAN
CALIFORNIAN	HOLLAND LOP
CHECKERED GIANT	JERSEY WOOLY
CHINCHILLA	LIONHEAD
DUTCH	MINI LOP
ENGLISH LOP	NEW ZEALAND
ENGLISH SPOT	PALOMINO
FLEMISH GIANT	POLISH
FLORIDA WHITE	REX
FRENCH LOP	SATIN

```
R E X R Z H F R E N C H L O P N
Z Z L I F R H O L L A N D L O P
Z O C F O C A L I F O R N I A N
U J B X L H A R L E Q U I N F V
H Z E A M E R I C A N S A B L E
I N L R J C M P O L I S H P O N
M E G A S K L I O N H E A D R G
A W I N S E A P S U F S I L I L
L Z A G D R Y M C H K U J F D I
A E N O U E S W I V G V I C A S
Y A H R T D Z A O N H I V Y W H
A L A A C G U B T O I R A A H S
N A R C H I N C H I L L A N I P
X N E L H A V A N A N Y O I T O
J D G T E N G L I S H L O P E T
D H R S G T P A L O M I N O S X
```

Answers on page 186.

BROKEN EGG

What number was painted on this egg before it was broken?

Answer on page 186.

SUDOKU

Use deductive logic to complete the grid so that each row, each column, and each 3 by 3 box contains the numbers 1 through 9 in some order. The solution is unique.

		4	3					
		1	2				7	
5	7	3	9	1				
6	3	5			2			
		8				6		
			6			4	8	5
				9	8	5	2	3
	4				3	9		
					7	8		

Answers on page 186.

WORD LADDER

Change just one letter on each line to go from the top word to the bottom word. Do not change the order of the letters. You must have a common English word at each step.

WHITE

_____

_____

_____

_____ (Salesman's products)

_____

_____

_____

DOVES

Answers on page 186.

PICTURE THIS

Place each of the 16 boxes in the 4 by 4 grid below so they form an Easter picture. Do this without cutting the page apart: Use only your eyes.

Answer on page 186.

SPRING FLOWERS

ACROSS

1. Tarzan's friends
5. Ending for cash or front
8. Corp. subdivision
12. Scottish hillside
13. Mississippi blossom
14. Frequent flyer
15. Sports stat.
16. Pinball error
17. One with removed limb
19. Smoothes the way
20. First part of the day
21. Potted miniature
23. Concise
27. Cape Town's country: abbr.
28. Ghostbusters goo
30. Pantry raid participant
31. Back to zero, say
33. Forewords
35. Souvenir
37. Gusto
40. Dionysian attendants
43. Cowboy's footwear
44. Playing marble
45. Wise guide
46. Wild hyacinth
47. Suffix with decor
48. Gym iterations
49. Start of a bray
50. Casual refusal

DOWN

1. "Dancing Queen" group
2. Cowslip
3. Legendary Wyatt
4. Creeping herbs
5. Put at risk
6. Swallowed
7. Some NFL linemen
8. Foolish affection
9. Students at New Haven
10. Heap of rubble
11. Makes lacework
18. One who offers good wishes
19. International alliance
21. Shivering sound
22. "Illmatic" rapper
24. Zipped file format

25. Early spring flower
26. Space visitors, briefly
29. Capable of being used as coal source
32. Shows feeling onstage
34. Friendly Islands native
36. Rat in "Ratatouille"

37. For short, for short
38. Performer's job
39. Decorate
41. Tune-up recipient
42. Yeah, right
44. Unenthusiastic response

1	2	3	4		5	6	7		8	9	10	11
12					13							
14					15				16			
17				18				19				
			20									
21		22						23		24	25	26
27				28			29			30		
31			32				33		34			
			35			36						
37	38	39				40				41		42
43				44				45				
46								47				
48				49				50				

Answers on page 186.

EASTER EQUALS

Below are several traditional Easter foods from around the globe. Match each food to its respective country.

1. Colomba di Pasqua

2. Defo Dabo

3. Fanesca

4. Kerbelsuppe

5. Le gigot d'agneau Pascal

6. Mämmi

7. Pinca

8. Tsoureki

A. Croatia

B. Ecuador

C. Ethiopia

D. Finland

E. France

F. Germany

G. Greece

H. Italy

Answers on page 186.

COMPLETE THE TALE

Below is a group of words that, when properly arranged in the blanks, reveal a quote from *The Tale of Peter Rabbit* by Beatrix Potter.

cousin   garden   pond   puzzled   twitched

Then he tried to find his way straight across the ____, but

he became more and more ____. Presently, he came to a

____ where Mr. McGregor filled his water-cans. A white cat

was staring at some gold-fish, she sat very, very still, but

now and then the tip of her tail ____ as if it were alive. Peter

thought it best to go away without speaking to her; he had

heard about cats from his ____, little Benjamin Bunny.

Answers on page 186.

EASTER ANAGRAM

The following phrases are all anagrams for the same term related to Easter. What is it?

A GIDDY ROOF

DIG FOOD RAY

FIG DAY DOOR

M_SS_NG V_W_LS

Below is a quote from *The Adventures of Peter Cottontail* by Thornton W. Burgess. The only thing is, some terms have lost A, E, I, O, and U, as well as any punctuation and spaces between words. Can you figure out the missing vowels and decipher each term?

"Why," said Peter Rabbit, when he could get his BRTH, "the joke is that the MNSTR that FRGHTND you so was the old straw hat of Farmer Brown's boy, and I was NDRNTH it. Ha, ha, ha! Ho, ho, ho!" Then Reddy Fox knew just how badly Peter Rabbit had fooled him. With a snarl he sprang right over the BRMBLBSH at Peter Rabbit, but Peter was watching and darted away along one of his own special little paths through the Old Briar-patch.

Answers on page 186.

LARGEST BUNNY HOP

Cryptograms are messages in substitution code. Break the code to read the message. For example, THE SMART CAT might become FVO QWGDF JGF if F is substituted for T, V for H, O for E, and so on.

Kbyrx, Drxg, acxiri rgb Jduppbii Lchyk Hbtchk

och rgb lchyk'i yxhjbir adppq gcn. Acppub

lgxwc, x tgxuhnbicp och Kbyrx'i tbprbppuxy

tbybahxrucp up 2007, gbynbk chjxpufb rgb

bmbpr rc gcpch Kbyrx Gujg Itgccy, lgcib wxitcr

ui rgb hxaaur. X hbtchk 3841 nxhrutunxpri

ochwbk cpb tcprupdcdi yupb up rgb wukkyb co

Wxup Irhbbr xpk adppq gcnnbk xlxq och x odyy

oumb wupdrbi. Kbyrx wchb rgxp kcdaybk rgb

nxir adppq gcn hbtchk co xacdr 1800 nbcnyb—

xpk kuk ic lurg cpyq x ncndyxrucp co xhcdpk

3100 nbcnyb. Xttchkupj rc *VIY Pbli*, rcdhuiri

muiurupj rgb rclp och rgb Ocdhrg co Sdyq

kbtukbk rc jbr upmcymbk, rcc.

CHICKEN BREEDS

Every word listed is contained within the group of letters. Words can be found in a straight line horizontally, vertically, or diagonally. They may be read either forward or backward.

AMERAUCANA

ANCONA

ARAUCANA

AUSTRALORP

BARNEVELDER

BRAHMA

COCHIN

DELAWARE

FAVEROLLES

FRIZZLE

LEGHORN

MARANS

MINORCA

NAKED NECK

NEW HAMPSHIRE RED

ORPINGTON

PLYMOUTH ROCK

POLISH

REDCAP

RHODE ISLAND RED

SEBRIGHT

SILKIE

SUSSEX

WYANDOTTE

```
O N W P B A R N E V E L D E R W
R E Y O R I U P J A N C O N A K
P W A P A S D S J M B M N P R R
I H N L H E I E T E J C G O A H
N A D Y M B O F L R E S J L U O
G M O M A R S A V A A O D I C D
T P T O R I P V S U W L W S A E
O S T U A G X E U C J A O H N I
N H E T N H T R S A O X R R A S
G I B H S T H O S N M C K E P L
A R F R I Z Z L E A I O H S E A
K E L O T Y P L X U N W K I D N
M R Y C C R L E G H O R N L N D
A E E K O W B S C W R I P K S R
Y D G L R E D C A P C X L I O E
N A K E D N E C K O A B N E Z D
```

Answers on page 187.

COMPLETE THE TALE

Below is a group of words that, when properly arranged in the blanks, reveal a quote from *The Tale of Peter Rabbit* by Beatrix Potter.

bushes   gate   noise   onions   wheelbarrow

He went back towards the tool-shed, but suddenly, quite close to him, he heard the ____ of a hoe—scr-r-ritch, scratch, scratch, scritch. Peter scuttered underneath the ____. But presently, as nothing happened, he came out, and climbed upon a ____ and peeped over. The first thing he saw was Mr. McGregor hoeing ____. His back was turned towards Peter, and beyond him was the ____!

   Answers on page 187.

EASTER IN NORWAY (PART I)

Read the story below, then turn the page and answer the questions.

You might think it strange to associate Easter—a time typically filled with imagery of bunnies, lambs, eggs, chocolate, and baskets—with gruesome crime stories and detective thrillers. Rest assured: The country of Norway has a perfectly logical explanation.

The tradition of *Påskekrim*, or "Easter crime," began in Norway just over 100 years ago when, according to the New York Public Library, in an "early display of viral marketing, a publisher took out a front-page ad in a newspaper with the title of the book it was promoting." With a title like *The Bergen Train Was Robbed in the Night*, however, readers of the paper began to mistakenly believe the actual Bergen train had been robbed. Instead of spending Easter week quietly in the comfort of family, Norwegians dove head-first into the mystery.

The tradition continues today. Every year, the entire country comes together to read, watch, and listen to stories of crime during the Easter holidays. Publishers bring out special editions of detective novels, bookstores and libraries set up large Påskekrim displays, radio and TV stations produce new murder mysteries—even milk companies contribute by printing short stories onto their milk cartons.

As uncharacteristic of an Easter tradition as it might be, it's comforting to see the people of Norway celebrate their love of mysteries together.

EASTER IN NORWAY (PART II)

(Do not read this until you have read the previous page!)

1. What does the Norwegian word *Påskekrim* translate to in English?
    A. Easter crime
    B. Easter detective
    C. Easter mystery
    D. Easter novel

2. What year did Norway's tradition of Påskekrim begin?
    A. 1907
    B. 1923
    C. 1954
    D. 1972

3. What was the name of the train featured in the title of the crime novel?
    A. Bergen
    B. Dovre
    C. Flåmsbana
    D. Flekkefjord

4. Every year at Easter, Norwegian bookstores and libraries set up large Påskekrim displays.
    _____ True
    _____ False

Answers on page 187.

PIC-A-PIX

Use the clues on the left of every row and the top of every column to reveal the picture hidden in the grid below. Numbers indicate how many blocks get colored in, and the sequence in which they get colored. There must be at least one empty square between each sequence.

Row clues (top to bottom):

- 6 1 7
- 2 2 1 2 3
- 1 1 1 1 4
- 1 1 3 4
- 1 4 1 2 1 1 2
- 2 2 4 2 2
- 2 3 2 1 3
- 6 2 2 2
- 3 2 3 1 1
- 2 3 2 1 2
- 1 1 2 1
- 1 3 2 1 1 2 2
- 2 1 3 1 1 4 1
- 1 5 1 3 1
- 1 9 1
- 2 1 2 2 2
- 3 1 3 3 3
- 6 3 1
- 2 13 5 1
- 1 3 5 2 1
- 1 4 4 1 8
- 2 3 2
- 2 2 5 3
- 3 3
- 6 4 6

Answer on page 187.

SHEEP BREEDS

Every word listed is contained within the group of letters. Words can be found in a straight line horizontally, vertically, or diagonally. They may be read either forward or backward.

CHAROLLAIS	MERINO
CHEVIOT	NAVAJO-CHURRO
COLUMBIA	POLYPAY
DORPER	RAMBOUILLET
DORSET	RIDEAU ARCOTT
FINNSHEEP	SHETLAND
HAMPSHIRE	SHROPSHIRE
ICELANDIC	SOAY
KARAKUL	SOUTHDOWN
KATAHDIN	SUFFOLK
LEICESTER LONGWOOL	TEXEL
LINCOLN	WELSH MOUNTAIN

```
K B X P X J Y S W L H A R K I S M L
A C G A J Q R I D E A U A R C O T T
R S U F F O L K Z I M J M P E U A E
A M T E X E L G X C P G B V L T R U
K E L N I C V J M E S E O H A H Z K
U R I D N H M Y S S H I U N N D S A
L I N N E A E H P T I W I L D O H T
P N C N O R V U I E R W L X I W E A
O O O U W O W A H R E J L Q C N T H
L F L F X L V Z J L Z B E O U U L D
Y I N W E L S H M O U N T A I N A I
P N J P D A T L L N C V D H I W N N
A N K D O I D A Z G L H X O V Y D R
Y S F R R S Y V P W T K U A R W Q X
G H G D S F E K O O T K I R H P N T
R E W D E J S H R O P S H I R E E T
P E R Y T A T A K L C H E V I O T R
Z P P C O L U M B I A I A S O A Y P
```

Answers on page 187.

EASTER ANAGRAM

The following phrases are all anagrams for the same term related to Easter. What is it?

BAKER ESTATES

BERATE SKATES

REBATE STEAKS

COMPLETE THE TALE

Below is a group of words that, when properly arranged in the blanks, reveal a quote from *The Tale of Peter Rabbit* by Beatrix Potter.

black-currant   fast   quietly   sight   underneath

Peter got down very ____ off the wheelbarrow; and started

running as ____ as he could go, along a straight walk behind

some ____ bushes. Mr. McGregor caught ____ of him at the

corner, but Peter did not care. He slipped ____ the gate, and

was safe at last in the wood outside the garden.

Answers on page 187.

EASTER MAZE

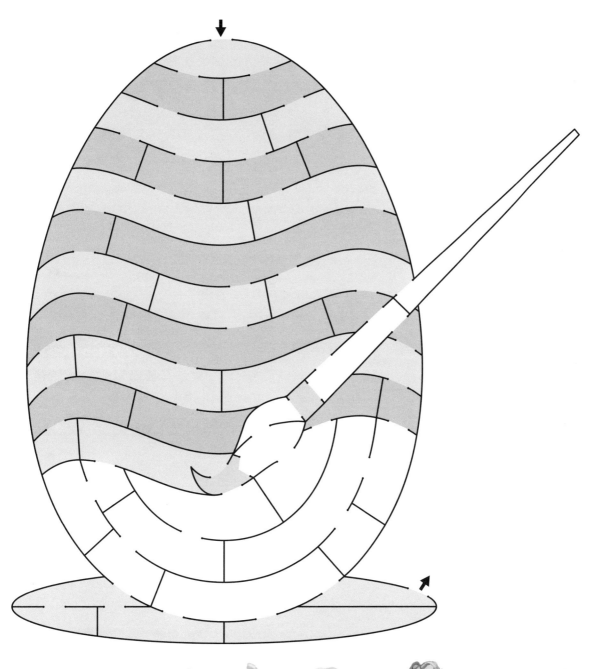

Answer on page 188.

WHAT'S INSIDE A CHOCOLATE BUNNY?

The words listed below can all be made from the letters in CHOCOLATE BUNNY. The words can be found in a straight line horizontally, vertically, or diagonally. They may read either forward or backward. When you've found all the words, the leftover letters will spell seven more words.

ACCENT	CLEAN-CUT	HOTEL
ANYONE	CLONE	LOONY
BALCONY	COCONUT	LUNCH
BALONEY	COUNTY	LUNCHEON
BEACH	CUTE	NOBLE
BEAUTY	CYCLE	NOTABLE
BOTANY	ENCHANT	TABLE
BOUNCE	HALO	TABOO
CANYON	HAUNT	TOUCH
CHANCE	HONEY	TUNNEL

Leftover letters:

_____

```
B H O N E Y A T H C H B O
A N O N B A L C O N Y Y C
C T B A B C U N Y H L E C
C U A Y L O L O E L A O T
E N T O T U H B N N C L C
N N N E N U C L O O N Y O
T E A C E O A E L T C E U
Y L H L C C H E A A A C N
C T C O L C H B B B N N T
O Y N N N C L A E L Y U Y
C U E U A E E C N E O O H
T C L E A N C U T C N B O
L U B N A H O T E L E C Y
```

WORD LADDER

Change just one letter on each line to go from the top word to the bottom word. Do not change the order of the letters. You must have a common English word at each step.

RAIN

____

____

____

____

____

____

____

COAT

Answers on page 188.

MORE THAN A DROP

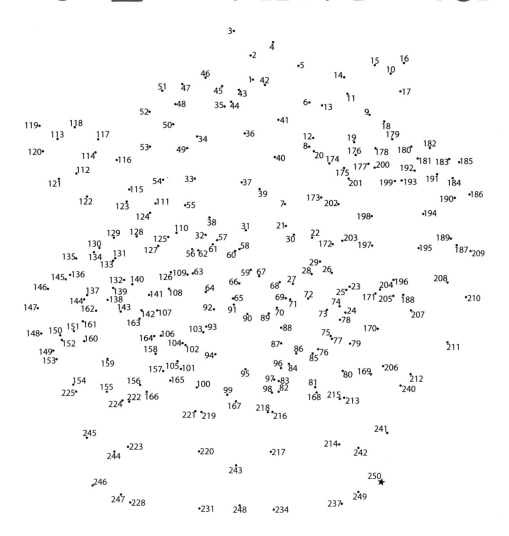

Answer on page 188.

LARGEST HOT CROSS BUN

Cryptograms are messages in substitution code. Break the code to read the message. For example, THE SMART CAT might become FVO QWGDF JGF if F is substituted for T, V for H, O for E, and so on.

Pxvjvozivoj vo icb Qovibl Avojlph, cpi kxpdd

fqod zxb devkbl fqod kpoizvovoj dhzrr evbkbd pt

txqvi, icb iped pt ncvkc zxb hzxabl nvic z kxpdd

hzlb pt trpqx ezdib. Opi zrr fqod zxb hzlb zrvab,

cpnbubx. Po Zexvr 5, 2012, icb Xpszr Dpkvbis

tpx icb Expibkivpo pt Fvxld (XDEF) npxabl vo

kpomqokivpo nvic Jxbboczrjcd Fzabxs vo Fpripo,

Qovibl Avojlph, ip kxbzib icb npxrl'd rzxjbdi cpi

kxpdd fqo. Qdvoj zrr ixzlvivpozr vojxblvboid—

vokrqlvoj 143.3 epqold pt trpqx—icb ibzh pt

dixpoj zol izrboibl fzabxd explqkbl z fqo nbvjcvoj

zo vhexbddvub 370 epqold. Iczi'd bwqvuzrboi ip

icb nbvjci pt 2300 xbjqrzx cpi kxpdd fqod!

Answers on page 188.

EASTER IN POLAND (PART I)

Read the story below, then turn the page and answer the questions.

Few things represent Easter better than a friendly water fight—at least in Poland. *Śmigus Dyngus*, also known as *Lany Poniedziałek*, or Wet Monday, is an Easter Monday tradition that involves soaking those around you with copious amounts of water. If you're out and about, beware: No one is safe.

The tradition reportedly recalls the baptism of Mieszko I, the first historical ruler of Poland who introduced Christianity into the country, on Easter Monday in 966—but it also echoes several pagan fertility rituals. The tradition is not limited to Poland, either. According to the website Culture.pl, similar Easter Monday rituals can be found all around Central and Eastern Europe, like in Slovakia, Hungary, and Ukraine. Diaspora groups outside the region often celebrate, too.

In the olden days, young women were the main target of the soaking as it was believed that, the more a girl was drenched with water, the higher her chances of getting married within the year. Nowadays, however, the tradition has expanded to include just about everyone. Generally, it is young people that participate the most—although the young at heart are free to join in on the chaos, should they choose. The weapons of choice range from water pistols to bottles, hoses, and especially buckets.

EASTER IN POLAND (PART II)

(Do not read this until you have read the previous page!)

1. What does *Lany Poniedziałek* translate to in English?
   A. Easter Baptism
   B. Soaking Ritual
   C. Water Sprinkle
   D. Wet Monday

2. What was the name of the first ruler of Poland?
   A. Bolesław I
   B. Lech
   C. Mieszko I
   D. Śmigus Dyngus

3. The more a girl was drenched, the higher her chances of getting married within the year.
   _____ True
   _____ False

4. Which of the following is not typically used in a water fight?
   A. bathtub
   B. bucket
   C. hose
   D. water pistol

Answers on page 188.

EASTER MAZE

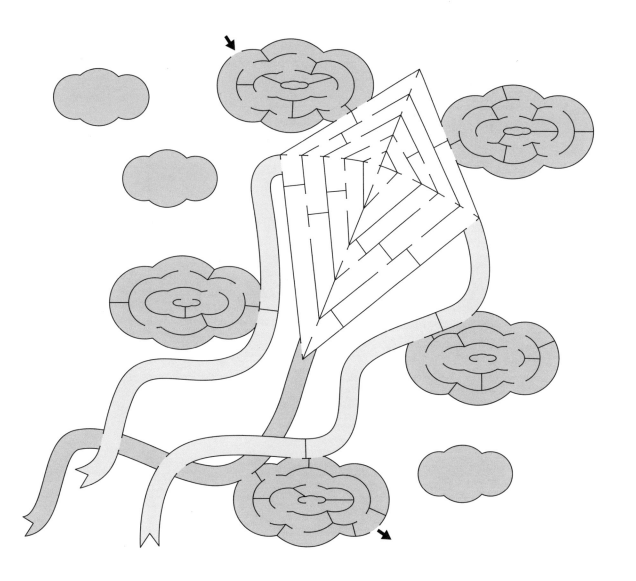

Answer on page 189.

M_SS_NG V_W_LS

Below is a quote from *The Adventures of Peter Cottontail* by Thornton W. Burgess. The only thing is, some terms have lost A, E, I, O, and U, as well as any punctuation and spaces between words. Can you figure out the missing vowels and decipher each term?

In the Old Briar-patch Peter was safe. Reddy had tried to FLLW him there, but he had found that it was of no use at all. Peter's paths were so NRRW, and the BRMBLS tore Reddy's clothes and SCRTCHD him so, that he had to give it up. Reddy was thinking of this one day as he sat on his door-step, SCWLNG over at the Old Briar-patch, and then all of a sudden he thought of Shadow the Weasel.

ALLERGY ADDAGRAM

This puzzle functions exactly like an anagram with an added step: In addition to being scrambled, each term below is missing the same letter. Discover the missing letter, then unscramble the words. When you do, you'll reveal 5 terms associated with spring allergies.

BEE GINS (two words)

COINS GONE

EDIT SUMS (two words)

IRON RAISIN KIT (two words)

LONER PEEL (two words)

Answers on page 189.

HEAVIEST & LARGEST CHICKEN EGGS

Cryptograms are messages in substitution code. Break the code to read the message. For example, THE SMART CAT might become FVO QWGDF JGF if **F** is substituted for **T**, **V** for **H**, **O** for **E**, and so on.

Sj Hvatkctx 25, 1956, zj Bzjvpcjy, Jvi Dvtovx, c Igzev Pvfgstj gvj pczy egv gvcbzvoe ngznuvj vff sj tvnsty: c 16 skjnv vff izeg c yskapv ogvpp cjy yskapv xspu. Ake egce ico hct htsr egv pctfvoe vff vbvt pczy. Cntsoo egv qsjy zj Vcoeissy, Okoovw, Esjx Actaskez sjnv sqvjvy gzo ngznuvj nssq es hzjy cj vff rvcoktzjf 9.1 zjngvo zj nztnkrhvtvjnv. Cpegskfg ze sjpx ivzfgvy cqqtswzrcevpx 5.68 skjnvo, egv gvj tvoqsjozapv ico ovvj icpuzjf c aze hkjjx hst c hvi ycxo chevtictyo, ake ossj tvnsbvtvy nsrqpvevpx.

WHAT'S INSIDE A JELLY BEAN?

Every word listed is contained within the group of letters. Words can be found in a straight line horizontally, vertically, or diagonally. They may be read either forward or backward.

ABLE	EEL
ALLEY	ENABLE
ALLY	EYEBALL
ANY	JAB
BALE	JEAN
BALEEN	JELL
BALL	LABEL
BAN	LANE
BAY	LAY
BELAY	LEAN
BELLY	LYE
BYE	YELL

```
N C K R L Y L L A M R G W J
F T O G E V O P L E B A L U
Y N Y N Z A E N A B L E N J
L J V L E Y E B A L L V A F
L A L Y R T K A N Y E R E T
E B E G E P B A R L L C L W
B B A Y L L E E A B E N K N
U B W E Z K L M Q Y A A L Y
G E B U N A B A F O H E E B
F E R A N Q J M L E A J L E
P N T L L H L F Q L Y L A L
Z A E U L E Q L P W E B B A
G L D E R A E D E Z H J U Y
M L Y E H S B N S Y K I I U
```

EASTER EQUALS

Below are several traditional Easter foods from around the globe. Match each food to its respective country.

1. Baked ham

2. Capirotada

3. Figolli

4. Hot cross buns

5. Pashka

6. Påskmust

7. Torrijas

8. Żurek

A. Malta

B. Mexico

C. Poland

D. Russia

E. Spain

F. Sweden

G. United Kingdom

H. United States

Answers on page 189.

WORD LADDER

Change just one letter on each line to go from the top word to the bottom word. Do not change the order of the letters. You must have a common English word at each step.

HOLY

____

____

____

____

DAYS

Answers on page 189.

ON THE LAMB

Answer on page 189.

BROKEN EGG

What number was painted on this egg before it was broken?

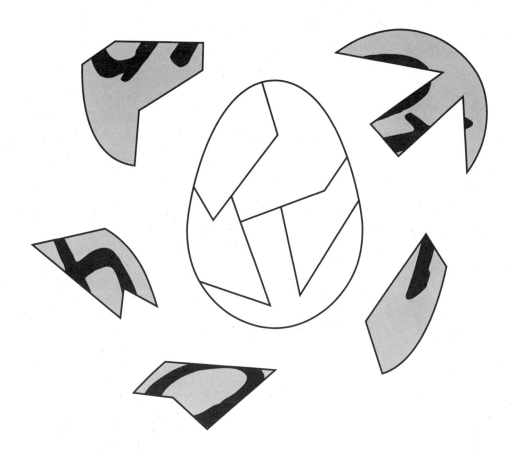

Answer on page 190.

SPRING ALLERGIES

ACROSS

1. Pekingese or Chihuahua
6. Comes up in the east
10. Hand cream enhancer
11. Utilities
13. One of the Tuvalu Islands
15. Bird with a forked tail
16. Sneeze-causing substance
18. Hellenic courtesan
19. Beaux-___
20. Damask rose oil
22. Caused by the wind
26. ___ Fernando Valley
28. Medicine used to treat reaction to pollen, e.g.
31. ACLU's concern: abbr.
32. Inspire to love
33. Oriental
35. The Goddess of Pop
38. Having fustier smell
42. Pollinosis
45. Ratio phrase
46. Ram's madam
47. Troll's relative
48. Home invaders
49. Reykjavik cash
50. Dakota Indian tribe

DOWN

1. Plaster base
2. Away from the win
3. Harbor city
4. Old Roman coins
5. Paraguayan currency and South American Indian language
6. Fam. member
7. Final ending, in England
8. M.I.T. grad, most likely
9. Winter treat for birds
12. Bed frame part
14. More nuts
17. Zipped file format
21. Strong-ox link
22. Otitis, familiarly
23. Thunder Bay's prov.
24. Mil. officers
25. Inventor's cries
26. ___City (old computer game)

27. Year in Rio
29. Lengths of service
30. Certain alien
33. Bark in comics
34. No. or So. continent
36. Sell with a yell

37. Observer
39. Exists no more
40. Kitchen suffix
41. Shade of red
43. Forever and a day
44. Very old computer display standard

Answers on page 190.

PICTURE THIS

Place each of the 20 boxes in the 4 by 5 grid below so they form an Easter picture.
Do this without cutting the page apart: Use only your eyes.

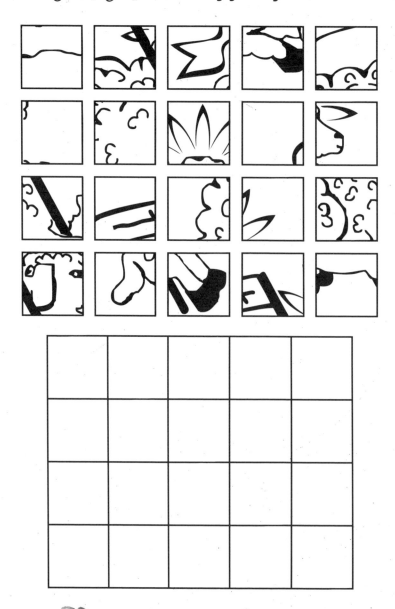

Answer on page 190.

COMPLETE THE TALE

Below is a group of words that, when properly arranged in the blanks, reveal a quote from *The Tale of Peter Rabbit* by Beatrix Potter.

blackbirds   fir-tree   rabbit-hole   sand   scare-crow

Mr. McGregor hung up the little jacket and the shoes for a

____ to frighten the ____. Peter never stopped running or

looked behind him till he got home to the big ____. He was

so tired that he flopped down upon the nice soft ____ on the

floor of the ____ and shut his eyes.

   Answers on page 190.

SUDOKU

Use deductive logic to complete the grid so that each row, each column, and each 3 by 3 box contains the numbers 1 through 9 in some order. The solution is unique.

8								9
			6	5	2			
	6		9		1		5	
	7	2	5		3	6	8	
	4			2			7	
	5	8	1		7	4	3	
	9		3		5		2	
			4	6	8			
7								3

Answers on page 190.

LARGEST (EASTER) BASKET

Cryptograms are messages in substitution code. Break the code to read the message. For example, THE SMART CAT might become FVO QWGDF JGF if F is substituted for T, V for H, O for E, and so on.

Gs aed 1990w, aed Yusncjdqndq Tuhrcsp, cs Chdqgtcs jqcsi lsuvs kuq gaw ecsitqckadi euhd idtuq rquiztaw, tuhhgwwgusdi c qcaedq zszwzcy ukkgtd jzgyigsn au jd zwdi cw aed tuhrcsp'w tuqruqcad edciozcqadqw gs Sdvcql, Uegu: c wdmds-wauqp jzgyigsn qdwdhjygsn c Yusncjdqndq hcrydvuui jcwlda. Jdtczwd uk gaw jcwlda wecrd— aed ycqndwa jcwlda gs aed vuqyi, su ydww—aed jzgyigsn'w zrrdq kyuuqw vdqd vgidq aecs aed kyuuqw jdyuv aedh. Ca aed aur, aed jcwlda ecsiydw vdgnedi sdcqyp 150 ausw csi tuzyi jd edcadi au rqdmdsa gtd kquh ichcngsn aed jzgyigsn izqgsn tuyidq vdcaedq. Jdavdds Rcyh Wzsicp csi Dcwadq Wzsicp, Yusncjdqndq ciidi ycqnd qdrygtc dnnw au aed aur uk aed jzgyigsn, aqcswkuqhgsn ga gsau aed vuqyi'w ycqndwa Dcwadq jcwlda.

EASTER ANAGRAM

The following phrases are all anagrams for the same term related to Easter. What is it?

BUSH CONSORT

HOT CORN SUBS

STUNS BROOCH

M_SS_NG V_W_LS

Below is a quote from *The Adventures of Peter Cottontail* by Thornton W. Burgess. The only thing is, some terms have lost A, E, I, O, and U, as well as any punctuation and spaces between words. Can you figure out the missing vowels and decipher each term?

Reddy's plan was very SMPL. Shadow the Weasel was to FLLW Peter Rabbit along Peter's narrow little PTHS and drive Peter out of the Old Briar-patch on to the GRNMDWS, where Reddy Fox could surely CTCH him. So Reddy Fox sat down to wait while Shadow started into the Old Briar-patch. Peter Rabbit heard him coming and, of course, Peter began to run.

Answers on page 190.

WORD LADDER

Change just one letter on each line to go from the top word to the bottom word. Do not change the order of the letters. You must have a common English word at each step.

FLOWER

_____

_____ (imperfect)

_____

_____

_____ (molded)

_____

_____ (phrased)

_____

_____ (prison boss)

GARDEN

Answers on page 191.

WHAT'S INSIDE A MARSHMALLOW PEEP?

The words listed below can all be made from the letters in MARSHMALLOW PEEP. The words can be found in a straight line horizontally, vertically, or diagonally. They may read either forward or backward. When you've found all the words, the leftover letters will spell eight more words.

AMPLE	MELLOW	SHAPEWEAR
APPEAL	PALM	SPAM
APPLE	PAMPELMOES	SWAMP
EMPOWER	PAMPER	SWAP
HAMMER	PLOW	WALLOP
HEMP	POMMEL	WALLPAPER
LAMP	ROSE	WHELM
MEALWORM	SHALLOW	WHOLESALE

Leftover letters:

_____

```
R O S E P A E R W A L L O P
O S H S E O L L A M S W P H
W O R H P A M P E R W H P S
H A H A A S A M L L A E L W
O W O P M P W M E A M L O A
L A L E P A A P R L P M W P
E L O W E M H E M P P P A L
S L S E L A M A A P P E A L
A P H A M P O E M P O W E R
L A A R O E R E P M P P H A
E P L L E A L R L A E L O P
E E L P S L O L E A L R E W
S R O M E A L W O R M M H A
R E W W H O L E M W E P A L
```

Answers on page 191.

EASTER MAZE

Answer on page 191.

EASTER IN SWEDEN (PART I)

Read the story below, then turn the page and answer the questions.

Visit Sweden during the springtime, and you might be surprised to see young children dressed as witches going door-to-door for some candy. It's not Halloween—it's actually Easter! On either the Thursday or Saturday before Easter—the custom varies slightly by region—young children continue a centuries-old tradition that harkens back to an old Swedish legend.

This tradition—celebrated in Finland as well as Sweden—sees both boys and girls painting their faces and donning headscarves, shawls, and long skirts to take on the disguise of the *Påskkärring*, or Easter Witch. They travel from house to house, wishing people a happy Easter and gifting drawings, paintings, or letters full of candy to their neighbors and friends. After their little excursion, the children are given *Påskägg*, or large eggs filled with candy and chocolate, by their parents.

The tradition comes from the old belief that witches flew on their broomsticks to a fictitious German island called Mount Blåkulla the Thursday before Easter, the day the apostle Judas betrayed Jesus. There, they would celebrate the Sabbath with the Devil. According to the legend, everything surrounding the mountain was upside down and backwards, and those who attended the celebration would partake in vulgar festivities and dancing. Then, the witches would return home on Easter Eve.

EASTER IN SWEDEN (PART II)

(Do not read this until you have read the previous page!)

1. Which of the following is one of the two possible days Swedish children dress up as Påskkärring witches?
   - A. Good Friday
   - B. Easter Saturday
   - C. Easter Sunday
   - D. Easter Monday

2. Besides Sweden, what other country celebrates this custom?
   - A. Estonia
   - B. Finland
   - C. Germany
   - D. Lithuania

3. Which of the following is NOT something the children gift their neighbors?
   - A. drawings
   - B. letters filled with candy
   - C. paintings
   - D. Påskägg eggs full of chocolate

4. The Easter Witch tradition comes from the old belief that witches flew on their broomsticks to visit the actual German island of Mount Blåkulla.
   - _____ True
   - _____ False

Answers on page 191.

COMPLETE THE TALE

Below is a group of words that, when properly arranged in the blanks, reveal a quote from *The Tale of Peter Rabbit* by Beatrix Potter.

bed-time   bread   clothes   evening   shoes

His mother was busy cooking; she wondered what he had done with his ____. It was the second little jacket and pair of ____ that Peter had lost in a fortnight! I am sorry to say that Peter was not very well during the ____. His mother put him to bed, and made some camomile tea; and she gave a dose of it to Peter! "One table-spoonful to be taken at ____." But Flopsy, Mopsy, and Cotton-tail had ____ and milk and blackberries for supper.

Answers on page 191.

EASTER CANDY

Every word listed is contained within the group of letters. Words can be found in a straight line horizontally, vertically, or diagonally. They may be read either forward or backward.

CADBURY CREME EGG

CADBURY MINI EGGS

FERRERO CRISPY EGG

JELLY BELLY JELLY BEANS

JORDAN ALMONDS

KINDER JOY EGG

KIT KAT LEMON CRISP

KNIPSCHILDT EASTER EGG

LINDT CHOCOLATE BUNNY

LINDT CHOCOLATE CARROT

MARSHMALLOW PEEP

NERDS ROPE

REESE'S PEANUT BUTTER BUNNY

REESE'S PEANUT BUTTER EGG

REESE'S PIECES CARROT

SOUR PATCH KIDS BUNNIES

STARBURST JELLY BEANS

SWEETARTS JELLY BEANS

TONY'S CHOCOLONELY EGG CARTON

WHOPPERS ROBIN EGGS

```
R E E S E S P E A N U T B U T T E R B U N N Y I K
J R R N X M R G Y F B U H M W D N F Q T V X M C H
T O N Y S C H O C O L O N E L Y E G G C A R T O N
L M L M D A P R J R I N P P U S N T T A F T V Y Q
Q U J T J V L K K W W W L T I A M B T V H D Z D R
S S O U R P A T C H K I D S B U N N I E S K S I E
W U R Q R L I N D T C H O C O L A T E B U N N Y E
M T D R Y R O K K I T K A T L E M O N C R I S P S
H C A D B U R Y M I N I E G G S W Q W W K P B L E
F A N Y D D C C F S N E D N N E F G J Z D S Q M S
H D A X Q Y T P G A V D R R S I Z Y D W R C E E P
R B L G B X F H J Q D B E D H G N Y E E M H Q I I
Q U M U K K G S G S H D Q R S A U K O K W I C R E
J R O Z F E R D D I B W I C J R O N H N J L V N C
Z Y N V G D Y N R U E C L U F O O L I N J D T T E
Y C D K H A F D Y V H E Q E N V Y P A I C T F L S
T R S M B F T H J H C F U H S I C E E S Z E P L C
F E R R E R O C R I S P Y E G G S G N I A C L A
L M A R S H M A L L O W P E E P S B E G E S P M R
J E L L Y B E L L Y J E L L Y B E A N S M T G H R
R E E S E S P E A N U T B U T T E R E G G E X U O
X G Z J T L I N D T C H O C O L A T E C A R R O T
P G Q W K F S T A R B U R S T J E L L Y B E A N S
K S W E E T A R T S J E L L Y B E A N S T G P Q N
C M A V I T N W H O P P E R S R O B I N E G G S Z
```

Answers on page 191.

BABY BUNNY

99 100
98• •101
76• •77
75• •78
74• •79 97• •102
•80 96• 95• •103
126★ •73 •81 94• •104
•82
125• •72 •83 93• •105
124• •71 •84 92• •106
•70 •85 91• •107
123• •69 •86
122• •68 •87 •90 •108
121•
120• •67 88★ •89
119• 50 49 48 •109
118• •66 •51
117• •110
65• ★52 •111
64• 112★ •47 222
63• 7 •46 •
62• 8★ 6 113• •45 221 220 219
1• 5 •44 • • 218
2• 3 4 114• •43 35 36 217
61• 21 115• 34 ★ •216
60• 22 116★ •42 •215
127• 23 27 •188 •214
128• 59• 24 •41 •213
129• 20 19 18 25 26 40 31 •212
130• 58• 37 38 •28 32 •189 211•
57 56 15 55 54 53 39 29 33 190 210• 186
131• 12 9 10 11 171★ •191 209• 187 •185
150★ •132 16 13 170• 30 192 208• •184
149• •133 17★ 14 169• •183
134 •151 168• 193 207• •182
148• 135 •152 167• 195 194 206• •181
147• 136 153 166• 197 196 205• •204
146• 137 138 154 165 176• 178 •203
145• 139 155 164 172 173 174 175 179 202
144• 140 156 163• 198• ★177 ★180 200 201
143 142 141 162• 199
157 161 160
158 159

168
Answer on page 191.

M_SS_NG V_W_LS

Below is a quote from *The Adventures of Peter Cottontail* by Thornton W. Burgess. The only thing is, some terms have lost A, E, I, O, and U, as well as any punctuation and spaces between words. Can you figure out the missing vowels and decipher each term?

Sammy Jay, looking around for MSCHF, found Reddy Fox sitting on his DRSTP with his chin in both hands and looking as if he hadn't a friend in the WRLD. "What are you doing?" asked Sammy Jay. "I'm just a-studying," replied Reddy Fox. "What are you STDYNG? Perhaps I can help you," said Sammy Jay. Reddy Fox HVD a long sigh. "I'm a-studying how I can catch Peter Rabbit," replied Reddy.

WORD LADDER

Change just one letter on each line to go from the top word to the bottom word. Do not change the order of the letters. You must have a common English word at each step.

GOOD

____

____

____

WILL

Answers on page 192.

BROKEN EGG

What number was painted on this egg before it was broken?

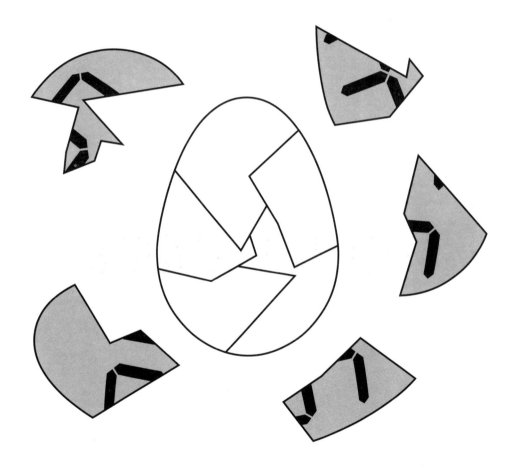

Answer on page 192.

EASTER ANAGRAM

The following phrases are all anagrams for the same term related to Easter. What is it?

NEARBY TUNES

SUNNY REBATE

UNBENT YEARS

WORD LADDER

Change just one letter on each line to go from the top word to the bottom word. Do not change the order of the letters. You must have a common English word at each step.

PINK

____

____

____

ROSE

Answers on page 192.

SUDOKU

Use deductive logic to complete the grid so that each row, each column, and each 3 by 3 box contains the numbers 1 through 9 in some order. The solution is unique.

9		3				6		1
			2	6	8			
6			1		3			5
	4	8	9		7	3	1	
	6						5	
	9	5	6		1	4	2	
4			8		6			3
			3	1	4			
1		6				7		8

Answers on page 192.

EASTER WORDPLAY

How many 5-letter words can you make by removing one letter at a time from EASTER and then rearranging the letters that remain? Remove an E, for example, and you might make STARE. How many others are there? We found at least 15.

____ ___ ___

____ ___ ___

____ ___ ___

____ ___ ___

____ ___ ___

Answers on page 192.

ANSWERS

LARGEST CHOCOLATE EGG (page 4)

The honor for creating the world's largest chocolate Easter egg on display goes to one chocolatier in Tosca, Italy. Made at the Le Acciaierie Shopping Centre in 2011, the confectionery egg measured 34 feet, 1.05 inches tall; had a circumference of 64 feet, 3.65 inches at its widest point; and weighed a whopping 15,873 pounds. To put that into perspective, that's several hundred pounds heavier than a full-grown male African savannah elephant. In addition to being the world's largest chocolate egg, it also holds the title as the world's tallest.

EASTER ANAGRAM (page 5)

Chocolate bunny

COMPLETE THE TALE (page 5)

four; Mother; sand-bank; very; fir-tree

SIGNS OF SPRING (pages 6-7)

Leftover letters spell: "Spring is nature's way of saying, 'Let's party!'"

–Robin Williams

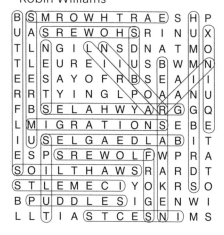

WORD LADDER (page 8)

Answers may vary. LAMB, lame, tame, tale, tall, TAIL

EASTER IN BERMUDA (pages 9-10)

1. B; 2. D; 3. True; 4. A

EASTER MAZE (page 11)

LARGEST EASTER EGG (page 12)

Situated between Salou and Tarragona in southern Catalonia, Spain, the PortAventura theme park is known for its six different worlds of adventure, as well as over 3 miles of roller coasters. It's also known for the world's largest decorated Easter egg, a title which it stole from Associacao Visite Pomerode's egg in Pomerode, Brazil, in March of 2022. Spain's unmissable, multicolored attraction features a range of bright blue, green, red, yellow, and gold patterns. It stands at approximately 52.43 feet tall, and measures 34.94 feet in diameter. While the egg is certainly impressive, it's entirely inedible.

M_SS_NG V_W_LS (page 13)

Mother Nature; common; laugh; anything; wonderful

GARDEN ADDAGRAM (page 13)

The missing letter is R.

Watering can; wheelbarrow; rake; sprinkler; trowel

BLOSSOMING SHRUBS & TREES
(pages 14-15)

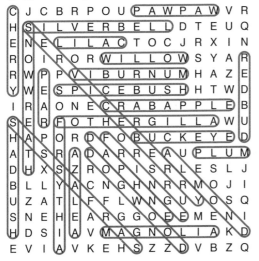

SPRING SURPRISE (page 16)

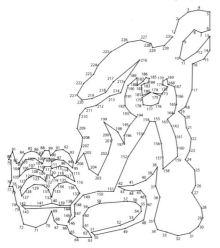

EASTER EQUALS (page 17)

1. A; 2. E; 3. B; 4. C; 5. D

BROKEN EGG (page 18)

WORD LADDER (page 19)

Answers may vary. EASTER, laster, lister, listed, lilted, lilied, LILIES

SEASONAL THEME (pages 20-21)

P	A	S	S			T	A	S	T	E
A	L	E	U	T		A	L	C	O	A
L	I	N	E	S		B	L	O	W	S
E	A	S	T	E	R	B	U	N	N	Y
S	S	E			H	E	R	E	S	
			C	L	Y	D	E			
	C	L	A	I	M			A	A	A
P	A	I	N	T	E	D	E	G	G	S
A	D	M	I	T		A	N	A	I	S
S	E	I	N	E		T	I	T	L	E
O	T	T	E	R		D	E	E	T	

PICTURE THIS (page 22)

WORD LADDER (page 23)

Answers may vary. WARM, ward, wand, WIND

COMPLETE THE TALE (page 23)

morning; fields; lane; garden; accident

SUDOKU (page 24)

7	9	6	1	2	4	3	5	8
3	1	4	8	7	5	2	6	9
5	2	8	6	9	3	7	1	4
8	6	1	7	4	2	9	3	5
9	4	7	3	5	6	1	8	2
2	3	5	9	1	8	4	7	6
1	7	2	5	8	9	6	4	3
4	5	3	2	6	7	8	9	1
6	8	9	4	3	1	5	2	7

LARGEST EASTER EGG HUNT (page 25)

The egg hunt is a classic Easter tradition, and for good reason: Children love looking for hidden decorated eggs and gathering them in baskets. While some hunts require searching through a backyard, other hunts are larger and made for the entire neighborhood to enjoy. But never has this been taken to such an extreme as on April 1, 2007, when the folks at the Cypress Gardens Adventure Park in Winter Haven, Florida, took it upon themselves to organize the world's largest Easter egg hunt. According to Guinness World Records, 9753 children and their parents searched for a whopping 501,000 eggs. Rumor has it that a number of undiscovered eggs might still be hiding in the Adventure Park's wilderness.

EASTER ANAGRAM (page 26)

Egg hunt

M_SS_NG V_W_LS (page 26)

somebody; friends; hereafter; kicked; pleased

PIC-A-PIX (page 27)

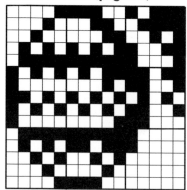

GARDEN TOOLS (pages 28-29)

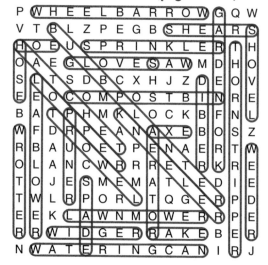

COMPLETE THE TALE (page 30)

mischief; umbrella; currant; blackberries; naughty

EASTER IN THE CZECH REPUBLIC (pages 31-32)

1. B; 2. C; 3. B; 4. True

EASTER MAZE (page 33)

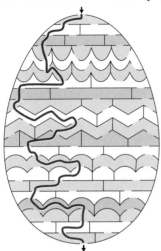

A SPRING BOUQUET (pages 34-35)

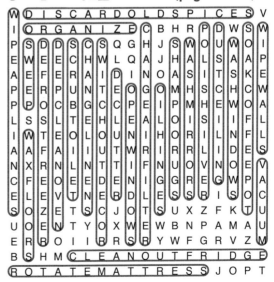

WORD LADDER (page 36)

Answers may vary. HOLY, hold, held, weld, weed, WEEK

LARGEST EASTER EGG TREE (page 37)

The tradition of decorating Easter egg trees has roots going back to Germany, where for centuries eggs have been hung on branches of outdoor trees and bushes using ribbon and thread. The tradition, called *Ostereierbaum*, is no longer limited to just Germany, however. On March 16, 2017, an Easter egg tree consisting of 82,404 painted hen eggs was achieved by Associacao Visite Pomerode to celebrate Osterfest in Pomerode, Santa Catarina, Brazil. Reportedly, it took almost an entire year to collect enough eggshells to decorate the tree and secure the Guinness World Record.

EASTER ANAGRAM (page 38)

Easter Sunday

COMPLETE THE TALE (page 38)

beans; radishes; sick; cucumber; meet

WORD LADDER (page 39)

Answers may vary. WINDY, winds, rinds, rands, raids, rains, RAINY

SPRING CLEANING (pages 40-41)

EASTER MAZE (page 42)

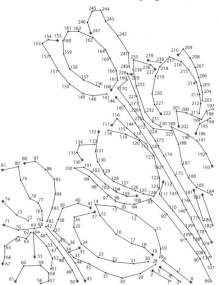

EASTER IN FRANCE
(pages 43-44)

1. B; 2. False; 3. D; 4. False

M_SS_NG V_W_LS (page 45)

chickens; breath; frightened; discovered; jumped

FLOWER ADDAGRAM (page 45)

The missing letter is A.

Azalea; bleeding heart; daffodil; forsythia; grape hyacinth

MOST EXPENSIVE CHOCOLATE EGG (page 46)

The Golden Speckled Egg wasn't the largest chocolate egg ever made, but it was certainly the most expensive. Created by William Curley and his team of 6 chocolatiers, the pricey egg was sculpted entirely from Amedei chocolate, which uses cocoa beans cultivated in the Chuao region of Venezuela. Inside the egg were truffles and couture chocolates, while the outside was decorated with 12 smaller chocolate eggs, 5 white flowers, 20 mini chocolate bars, and gold leaf. It took three days to make. The Golden Speckled Egg sold at t Royal Courts of Justice, London, on March 20th, 2012, for £7000. It weighed more than 110 pounds, and was approximately 3 feet, 6.13 inches tall and 1 foot, 9.26 inches wide.

THINK SPRING (page 47)

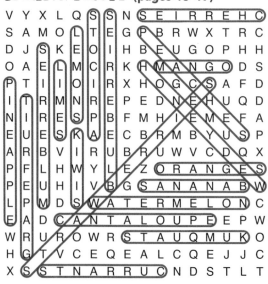

SPRING FRUIT (pages 48-49)

BROKEN EGG (page 50)

EASTER EQUALS (page 51)

1. A; 2. E; 3. D; 4. C; 5. B

EASTER RIDDLES (pages 52-53)

A	F	T	A	■	O	S	H	E	A	■	A	B	B	A
C	L	A	M	■	P	I	O	N	S	■	D	Y	E	D
H	A	R	E	R	O	B	I	C	S	■	O	H	I	O
E	M	O	T	E	S	■	L	A	B	R	A	T	S	
■	■	H	E	S	S	E	■	N	L	E	R	■	■	
C	I	T	Y	D	U	M	P	■	T	V	S	E	T	S
O	C	H	S	■	M	A	I	M	E	D	■	M	R	E
M	O	E	T	■	S	T	A	■	G	A	I	T		
E	N	O	■	B	A	H	A	M	A	■	A	I	N	U
T	S	U	R	I	S	■	P	I	N	K	S	L	I	P
■	T	O	E	S	■	H	E	G	E	L	■	■		
A	U	S	T	R	I	A	■	R	E	I	L	L	Y	
I	N	I	T	■	G	N	A	W	I	N	G	Y	O	U
R	I	D	E	■	N	A	V	A	L	■	H	O	O	K
S	T	E	N	■	S	T	A	C	Y	■	T	N	T	S

WORD LADDER (page 54)

Answers may vary. RAINY, rains, rails, fails, falls, walls, WALKS

PICTURE THIS (page 55)

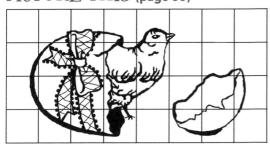

WORD LADDER (page 56)

Answers may vary. HOP, top, toy, JOY

COMPLETE THE TALE (page 56)

hands; thief; frightened; forgotten; gate

SUDOKU (page 57)

2	5	9	3	7	6	8	4	1
1	3	7	2	4	8	9	6	5
8	6	4	1	9	5	7	3	2
6	9	5	7	2	3	1	8	4
4	7	1	8	6	9	5	2	3
3	8	2	4	5	1	6	9	7
9	4	8	5	3	7	2	1	6
5	1	3	6	8	2	4	7	9
7	2	6	9	1	4	3	5	8

EASTER FOOD (pages 58-59)

V	N	D	C	W	T	H	Y	E	S	E	E	H	C	A	X
V	K	G	A	I	I	O	A	L	L	U	P	S	I	T	S
N	B	N	B	I	N	X	R	U	C	E	D	G	K	I	T
K	I	I	B	D	R	W	F	R	I	U	A	G	I	P	U
J	R	R	A	H	O	G	W	G	I	T	Y	E	Z	O	F
N	N	R	G	U	C	U	O	Q	B	J	B	V	T	K	F
Z	E	E	E	K	S	R	G	K	H	M	A	L	A	A	I
A	L	H	Y	X	E	O	K	H	A	U	J	S	Z	N	N
U	L	D	R	I	D	A	X	L	N	V	E	I	T	A	G
A	E	E	P	U	V	M	I	A	S	U	D	J	L	P	N
T	Z	L	E	M	O	N	P	O	T	A	T	O	E	S	L
B	Z	K	A	S	P	A	R	A	G	U	S	S	O	J	Z
A	I	C	A	R	R	O	T	C	A	K	E	Q	Z	S	X
B	P	I	D	T	V	V	X	U	U	I	J	M	A	H	Z
K	P	P	A	S	C	U	A	L	I	N	A	N	U	R	Z
A	Q	P	V	G	P	S	E	K	A	C	H	S	I	F	H

EASTER ANAGRAM (page 60)

Easter bonnet

179

M_SS_NG V_W_LS (page 60)

polite; pardon; mistake; breakfast; victim

EASTER MAZE (page 61)

PIC-A-PIX (page 62)

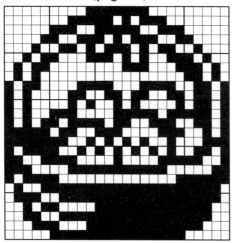

EASTER IN GREECE (pages 63-64)

1. D; 2. A; 3. C; 4. False

COMPLETE THE TALE (page 65)

cabbages; shoe; gooseberry; jacket; brass

EASTER BASKET TREATS
(pages 66-67)

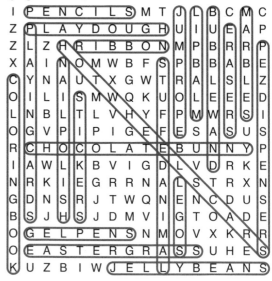

MOST EXPENSIVE CHOCOLATE RABBIT (page 68)

Chocolatiers come up with elaborate edible creations throughout the year, and Easter is no exception. In 2015, world-renowned confectioner and former chef of Harrods, Martin Chiffers, worked in collaboration with the company 77 Diamonds to create the world's most extravagant chocolate Easter bunny. Chiffers spent two-and-a-half 16-hour days carefully tempering, bonding, and carving 75% single origin Tanzanian chocolate into the shape of a rabbit 1 foot, 3 inches tall. Its eyes were inlaid with two shining diamonds. Three solid chocolate eggs covered in gold leaf sat at its base. The chocolate rabbit had approximately 548,000 calories—but with an equally hefty price tag of $63,000, you wouldn't be too tempted to take a bite.

COMPLETE THE TALE (page 69)

shed; sparrows; exert; sieve; water

LARGEST CHOCOLATE RABBIT
(page 70)

Although not quite as tall as the world's largest chocolate egg, the world's largest rabbit made from chocolate was still a sight to behold! Created on February 25, 2017, by Equipe da Casa do Chocolate at Shopping Uberaba in Uberaba, Minas Gerais, Brazil, the gargantuan bunny weighed 9359.7 pounds. It measured approximately 14 feet, 8 inches tall; had a width of 6 feet, 9 inches at its widest point; and was nearly 5 feet, 8 inches long. A total of 9 chocolatiering professionals worked over 8 consecutive days to create the rabbit sculpture. The previous holder of the record, Duracell South Africa in March 2010, created a bunny that measured approximately 12 feet tall.

BARROW OF FLOWERS **(page 71)**

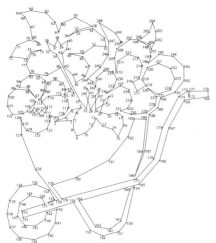

WORD LADDER **(page 72)**

Answers may vary. ROSE, rise, wise, wide, bide, bids, BUDS

EASTER IN GUATEMALA
(pages 73-74)

1. A; 2. D; 3. False; 4. False

EASTER MAZE **(page 75)**

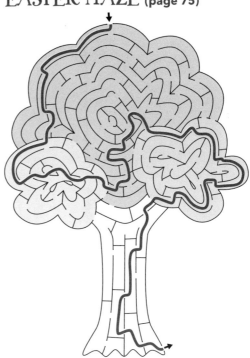

THINGS FOUND IN EASTER EGGS **(pages 76-77)**

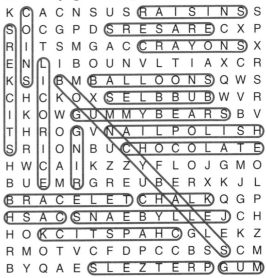

M_SS_NG V_W_LS **(page 78)**

hunting; appetite; chicken; trout; rabbit

CANDY ADDAGRAM (page 78)

The missing letter is E.

Reese's Pieces Carrot; Lindt Chocolate Bunny; Cadbury Creme Egg; Marshmallow Peep; Whoppers Robin Eggs

LARGEST RABBIT (page 79)

Flemish Giant rabbits are the largest breed of domestic rabbit and, historically, were kept as a utility breed for their fur and meat. Because of their docile and patient nature, today they are often kept as pets. These gentle giants typically weigh between 15 to 20 pounds, reaching lengths of about 2.5 to 4 feet when fully stretched out. One Flemish giant rabbit, however, set a new record for its species: Darius, owned by Annette Edwards in the United Kingdom, was found to weigh 49 pounds and measured a full 4 feet, 3 inches long.

EGG-CELLENT (pages 80-81)

Leftover letters spell: EGGS BENEDICT, HAM AND EGGS, EGG YOLK

EASTER EQUALS (page 82)

1. D; 2. A; 3. G; 4. C; 5. E; 6. H; 7. F; 8. B

FLOWERS & BOOTS (page 83)

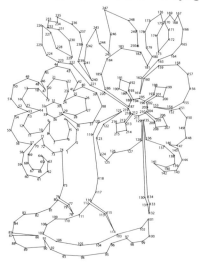

WORD LADDER (page 84)

Answers may vary. CANDY, sandy, sands, sends, seeds, seeps, PEEPS

BROKEN EGG (page 85)

PICTURE THIS (page 86)

EARLIEST HOLLOW CHOCOLATE EGG (page 87)

Covered in bright and patterned foil and packed into a box, chocolate Easter eggs might seem like a pretty recent invention—but think again! The earliest hollow chocolate eggs were produced in the United Kingdom by Fry's, a family-owned company, back in 1873. France and Germany had sold solid chocolate eggs for some time before, but it wasn't until Fry's figured out how to separate cocoa butter from the cocoa bean that the new, hollow delicacy took off. Fry's competitors quickly caught on to the trend and, two years later, the first Cadbury Easter Eggs were created.

BREAK TIME (pages 88-89)

H	A	T	S		B	A	G		C	I	O
E	P	E	E		U	R	U		I	N	B
L	I	R	A		R	E	R	I	N	S	E
E	A	S	T	E	R	S	U	N	D	A	Y
N	N	E		M	O	O		B	E	N	E
		N	I	S		O	A	R	E	D	
C	A	P	E	R		E	L	D			
A	M	A	H		A	R	A		D	A	B
F	O	U	R	T	H	O	F	J	U	L	Y
T	E	N	U	R	E	D		O	B	I	T
A	B	C		U	A	E		L	A	K	E
N	A	H		E	D	S		T	I	E	S

PIC-A-PIX (page 90)

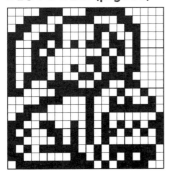

EASTER ANAGRAM (page 91)

Jelly bean

M_SS_NG V_W_LS (page 91)

middle; hurried; clover; chuckled; stomach

JELLY BEAN FLAVORS (pages 92-93)

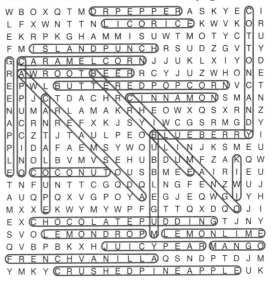

SUDOKU (page 94)

8	1	2	6	7	4	9	3	5
5	6	4	3	8	9	7	2	1
9	3	7	5	2	1	6	4	8
2	8	5	9	4	7	3	1	6
4	9	3	1	5	6	8	7	2
6	7	1	8	3	2	4	5	9
7	5	6	4	1	8	2	9	3
3	2	8	7	9	5	1	6	4
1	4	9	2	6	3	5	8	7

COMPLETE THE TALE (page 95)

tool-shed; flower-pot; carefully; sneezed; tried

EASTER MAZE (page 96)

EASTER IN HUNGARY
(pages 97-98)

1. D; 2. A; 3. True; 4. B

COMPLETE THE TALE (page 99)

window; running; trembling; idea; can

MORE JELLY BEAN FLAVORS
(pages 100-101)

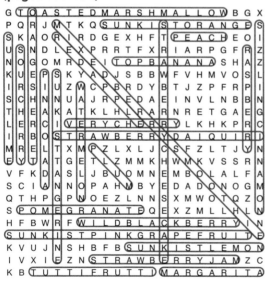

BLOOM WHERE YOU'RE PLANTED (page 102)

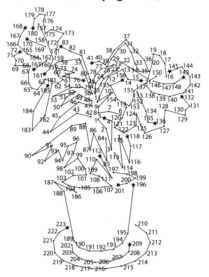

EASTER ANAGRAM (page 103)

Easter lily

COMPLETE THE TALE (page 103)

door; stone; wood; gate; answer

LONGEST LINE OF CHOCOLATE EGGS (page 104)

The world record for the longest line of chocolate eggs was achieved on April 16, 2017, by Santosh Singh Rawat and his talented team at the JW Marriott Mumbai Sahar in Mumbai, India. Although the 20,203 chocolate eggs might not have been considered noteworthy individually, put together they measured a total distance of 1026 meters, or 3366.14 feet. Following the conclusion of the record attempt, the chocolate eggs were displayed for sale.

WORD LADDER (page 105)

Answers may vary. GREEN, greed, treed, trees, tress, cress, crass, GRASS

FAMOUS BUNNIES (pages 106-107)

```
N A B R O Y N N U B R E Z I G R E N E U
E T N Y C B I C N P E T E R R A B B I T E
S T Y O S U E A S T E R B U N N Y M I L L
Q U I T C C I P O N T I B B A R R E G O R
U K I B H E C T C L A C O L A R E T E B F N U H
I R B B R E R T I B B A R R E R B O N O I E
K A B A R X T B S N A A R A E M V O A B I D Y
R B N X I B N E C F T H A R E F I O L R R N
A B E I T A N E A A H N A S Y T G F E E R A
B E R T N R C A B O N C W H Y E D D R H
B T R B I R R B B B N T I U T W R N E
E T I I A O I A U U G T C H E P A A T
R E T M D T O B P E G D O P E G D O H
E V O P L H E E S E A T S M C F I R S T
T L A M A A L P B Z I N U B G R L Y S T
E E V R E T E N U T Y H S I U X E P E A
R V C T E N N T O F P E N O T P A R
L E I P S T A N R T W I T H T N H E E
Y E L Y N N U B Y R U B D A C A R Y S P
```

M_SS_NG V_W_LS (page 108)

straight; straw hat; covered; strange; cabbage

CLEANING ADDAGRAM (page 108)

The missing letter is O.

Scrub toilet; deep clean oven; oil hinges; organize silverware; shampoo rugs

EASTER IN MEXICO (pages 109-110)

1. False; 2. D; 3. C; 4. True

MOST ENTRANTS IN AN EGG HUNT (page 111)

The most entrants in an egg hunt competition was achieved by the Faberge Big Egg Hunt, which was a 2012 charity fundraising campaign sponsored by the jeweler Faberge. Approximately 200 artists, celebrities, and designers were commissioned to create and paint large fiberglass eggs, which were then placed in selected locations throughout London. Beginning February 21, 12,773 participants had 40 days to locate the various giant eggs located around the capital. According to Faberge's website, the winner of the egg hunt—who chose to remain anonymous—was given the Jubilee Egg Prize: a rose gold, diamond, and precious stone Faberge egg worth £100,000. The Big Egg Hunt raised over £1 million for two charities—and set a world record in the process!

EASTER MAZE (page 112)

A HARE TO THE LEFT (page 113)

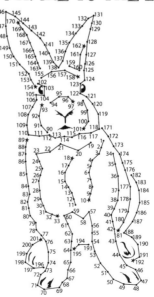

BUNNY BREEDS (pages 114–115)

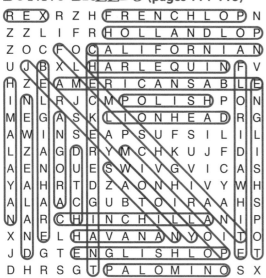

BROKEN EGG (page 116)

18

SUDOKU (page 117)

2	8	4	3	7	6	1	5	9
9	6	1	2	8	5	3	7	4
5	7	3	9	1	4	2	6	8
6	3	5	8	4	2	7	9	1
4	9	8	7	5	1	6	3	2
1	2	7	6	3	9	4	8	5
7	1	6	4	9	8	5	2	3
8	4	2	5	6	3	9	1	7
3	5	9	1	2	7	8	4	6

WORD LADDER (page 118)

Answers may vary. WHITE, whits, waits, warts, wares, cares, cores, coves, DOVES

PICTURE THIS (page 119)

SPRING FLOWERS (pages 120–121)

A	P	E	S		I	E	R		D	E	P	T
B	R	A	E		M	A	G	N	O	L	I	A
B	I	R	D		P	T	S		T	I	L	T
A	M	P	U	T	E	E		E	A	S	E	S
	R		M	O	R	N	I	N	G			
B	O	N	S	A	I			T	E	R	S	E
R	S	A		S	L	I	M	E		A	N	T
R	E	S	E	T		I	N	T	R	O	S	
			M	E	M	E	N	T	O		W	
A	R	D	O	R		M	A	E	N	A	D	S
B	O	O	T		M	I	B		G	U	R	U
B	L	U	E	B	E	L	L		A	T	O	R
R	E	P	S		H	E	E		N	O	P	E

EASTER EQUALS (page 122)

1. H; 2. C; 3. B; 4. F; 5. E; 6. D; 7. A; 8. G

COMPLETE THE TALE (page 123)

garden; puzzled; pond; twitched; cousin

EASTER ANAGRAM (page 124)

Good Friday

M_SS_NG V_W_LS (page 124)

breath; monster; frightened; underneath; bramble bush

LARGEST BUNNY HOP (page 125)

Delta, Utah, boasts the Guinness World Record for the world's largest bunny hop. Bonnie Shamo, a chairperson for Delta's centennial celebration in 2007, helped organize the event to honor Delta High School, whose mascot is the rabbit. A record 3841 participants formed one continuous line in the middle of Main Street and bunny hopped away for a full five minutes. Delta more than doubled the past bunny hop record of about 1800 people—and did so with only a population of around 3100 people. According to *KSL News*, tourists visiting the town for the Fourth of July decided to get involved, too.

PIC-A-PIX (page 131)

CHICKEN BREEDS (pages 126-127)

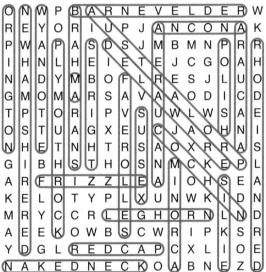

SHEEP BREEDS (pages 132-133)

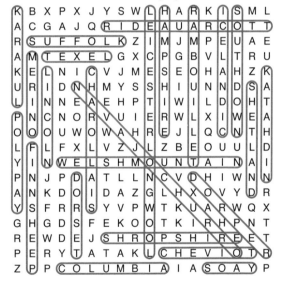

COMPLETE THE TALE (page 128)

noise; bushes; wheelbarrow; onions; gate

EASTER IN NORWAY (pages 129-130)

1. A; 2. B; 3. A; 4. True

EASTER ANAGRAM (page 134)

Easter basket

COMPLETE THE TALE (page 134)

quietly; fast; black-currant; sight; underneath

EASTER MAZE (page 135)

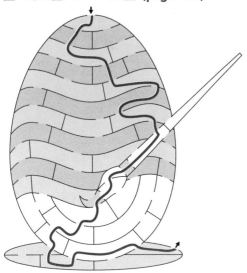

MORE THAN A DROP (page 139)

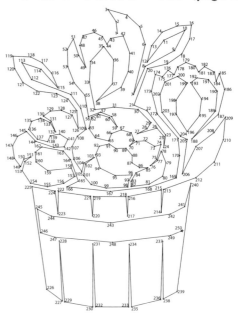

WHAT'S INSIDE A CHOCOLATE BUNNY? (pages 136-137)

Leftover letters spell: BATCH, BONNY, CABLE, CLOTH, CYCLONE, ECHO, LUNACY

LARGEST HOT CROSS BUN (page 140)

Originating in the United Kingdom, hot cross buns are spiced buns containing small pieces of fruit, the tops of which are marked with a cross made of flour paste. Not all buns are made alike, however. On April 5, 2012, the Royal Society for the Protection of Birds (RSPB) worked in conjunction with Greenhalghs Bakery in Bolton, United Kingdom, to create the world's largest hot cross bun. Using all traditional ingredients—including 143.3 pounds of flour—the team of strong and talented bakers produced a bun weighing an impressive 370 pounds. That's equivalent to the weight of 2300 regular hot cross buns!

EASTER IN POLAND (pages 141-142)

1. D; 2. C; 3. True; 4. A

WORD LADDER (page 138)

Answers may vary. RAIN, rail, tail, tall, toll, tool, cool, coal, COAT

188

EASTER MAZE (page 143)

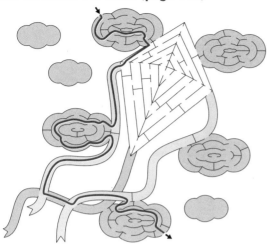

WHAT'S INSIDE A JELLY BEAN? (pages 146-147)

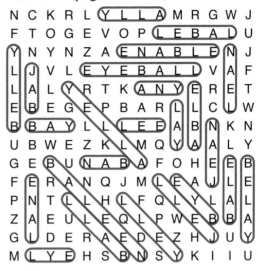

M_SS_NG V_W_LS (page 144)

follow; narrow; brambles; scratched; scowling

ALLERGY ADDAGRAM (page 144)

The missing letter is T.

Bee sting; congestion; dust mites; skin irritation; tree pollen

HEAVIEST & LARGEST CHICKEN EGGS (page 145)

On February 25, 1956, in Vineland, New Jersey, a White Leghorn hen laid the heaviest chicken egg on record: a 16 ounce egg with a double shell and double yolk. But that was far from the largest egg ever laid. Across the pond in Eastwood, Sussex, Tony Barbouti once opened his chicken coop to find an egg measuring 9.1 inches in circumference. Although it only weighed approximately 5.68 ounces, the hen responsible was seen walking a bit funny for a few days afterwards, but soon recovered completely.

EASTER EQUALS (page 148)

1. H; 2. B; 3. A; 4. G; 5. D; 6. F; 7. E; 8. C

WORD LADDER (page 149)

Answers may vary. HOLY, hole, hale, dale, dame, dams, DAYS

ON THE LAMB (page 150)

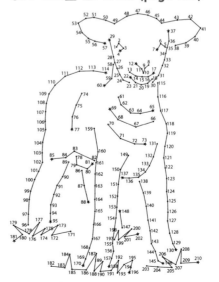

BROKEN EGG (page 151)

SPRING ALLERGIES (pages 152-153)

L	A	P	D	O	G		R	I	S	E	S	
A	L	O	E		U	S	E	S		N	U	I
T	E	R	N		A	L	L	E	R	G	E	N
H	E	T	A	E	R	A		A	R	T	S	
		R		A	T	T	A	R			S	A
E	O	L	I	A	N		S		S	A	N	
A	N	T	I	H	I	S	T	A	M	I	N	E
R	T	S		A		E	N	A	M	O	R	
A			A	S	I	A	N		R			
C	H	E	R			M	U	S	T	I	E	R
H	A	Y	F	E	V	E	R		I	S	T	O
E	W	E		O	G	R	E		A	N	T	S
	K	R	O	N	A		S	A	N	T	E	E

PICTURE THIS (page 154)

COMPLETE THE TALE (page 155)

scare-crow; blackbirds; fir-tree; sand; rabbit-hole

SUDOKU (page 156)

8	1	5	7	3	4	2	6	9
4	3	9	6	5	2	7	1	8
2	6	7	9	8	1	3	5	4
9	7	2	5	4	3	6	8	1
3	4	1	8	2	6	9	7	5
6	5	8	1	9	7	4	3	2
1	9	4	3	7	5	8	2	6
5	2	3	4	6	8	1	9	7
7	8	6	2	1	9	5	4	3

LARGEST (EASTER) BASKET (page 157)

In the 1990s, the Longaberger Company, an American brand known for its handcrafted home decor products, commissioned a rather unusual office building to be used as the company's corporate headquarters in Newark, Ohio: a seven-story building resembling a Longaberger maplewood basket. Because of its basket shape—the largest basket in the world, no less—the building's upper floors were wider than the floors below them. At the top, the basket handles weighed nearly 150 tons and could be heated to prevent ice from damaging the building during colder weather. Between Palm Sunday and Easter Sunday, Longaberger added large replica eggs to the top of the building, transforming it into the world's largest Easter basket.

EASTER ANAGRAM (page 158)

Hot cross bun

M_SS_NG V_W_LS (page 158)

simple; follow; paths, Green Meadows; catch

WORD LADDER (page 159)

Answers may vary. FLOWER, flowed, flawed, flamed, foamed, formed, forded, worded, warded, warden, GARDEN

WHAT'S INSIDE A MARSHMALLOW PEEP?
(pages 160-161)

Leftover letters spell: AEROSHELL, AMPHORA, HALLOW, MALAPROP, PALAMPORE, PHALAROPE, PLOWSHARE, WHOLEMEAL

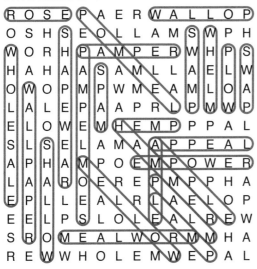

EASTER MAZE (page 162)

EASTER IN SWEDEN
(pages 163-164)

1. B; 2. B; 3. D; 4. False

COMPLETE THE TALE (page 165)

clothes; shoes; evening; bed-time; bread

EASTER CANDY (pages 166-167)

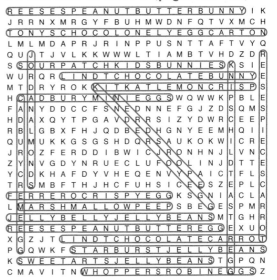

BABY BUNNY (page 168)

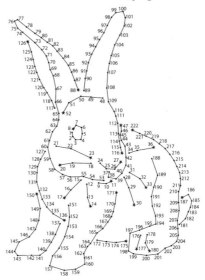

M_SS_NG V_W_LS (page 169)

mischief; door-step; world; studying; heaved

WORD LADDER (page 169)

Answers may vary. GOOD, gold, gild, wild, WILL

BROKEN EGG (page 170)

EASTER ANAGRAM (page 171)

Easter bunny

WORD LADDER (page 171)

Answers may vary. PINK, rink, risk, rise, ROSE

SUDOKU (page 172)

9	2	3	7	4	5	6	8	1
5	1	7	2	6	8	9	3	4
6	8	4	1	9	3	2	7	5
2	4	8	9	5	7	3	1	6
7	6	1	4	3	2	8	5	9
3	9	5	6	8	1	4	2	7
4	5	2	8	7	6	1	9	3
8	7	9	3	1	4	5	6	2
1	3	6	5	2	9	7	4	8

EASTER WORDPLAY (page 173)

aster, easer, eater, erase, ester, rates, reset, stare, steer, tares, taser, tears, tease, terse, trees